EPHESIANS

THE MYSTERY OF
THE CHURCH

EPHESIANS

THE MYSTERY OF THE CHURCH

12932

A Commentary by
William MacDonald

HAROLD SHAW · PUBLISHERS · WHEATON · ILLINOIS

Printed in the United States of America

CONTENTS

ABBREVIATIONS

ASV	American Standard Version (1901)
AV	Authorized Version
FWG	Numerical Bible, F. W. Grant
JBP	The New Testament in Modern English, J. B. Phillips
JND	The Holy Scriptures, A New Translation from the Original Languages, J. N. Darby
KSW	Expanded Translation of the Greek New Testament, Kenneth S. Wuest
NASB	New American Standard Bible
NEB	New English Bible
RSV	Revised Standard Version
RV	English Revised Version (1881)

Unless otherwise indicated, quotations are from the Authorized Version.

INTRODUCTION

The main subject of this letter is what Paul calls the mystery. By that he does not mean something that cannot be explained. Rather he means a wonderful truth that was never known before but that has now been revealed.

What is this wonderful truth which forms the theme of the Ephesian epistle? It is the announcement that believing Jews and believing Gentiles are now one in Christ Jesus. They are fellow members of the church, the body of Christ. At the present time they are seated in Him in heavenly places. In the future they will share His glory as Head over all things.

This mystery is found in each chapter of the letter.

In chapter 1 it is called the mystery of God's will, and looks forward to the time when all things in heaven and on earth will be headed up in Christ (vv. 9-10). Believing Jews (v. 11, "we") and believing Gentiles (v. 13, "ye") will have their share in the glory of that day. They will reign with Him over all the universe as His body and His fullness (vv. 22-23).

Chapter 2 describes the process by which Jews and Gentiles are saved by the grace of God; how they are reconciled to God and to one another; how, in union with Christ, they become one new man; and how they form a holy temple in which God dwells by His Spirit.

Chapter 3 gives the most complete explanation of the mystery. There it is spoken of as the mystery of the Christ (v. 4, JND), meaning Christ, the Head, and all believers, His body. In this body, believing Gentiles are fellow heirs, fellow members and fellow partakers of God's promise (v. 6).

Chapter 4 emphasizes the unity of the body and God's plan for its growth to maturity (vv. 1-16).

In chapter 5, the mystery is called Christ and the church (v. 32). The relationship between Christ and the church is the pattern for the relationship between a believing husband and wife.

Finally, in chapter 6 Paul speaks of the mystery of the gospel, for which he was an ambassador in bonds (v. 20).

Try to imagine the impact of this news on the Gentile believers to whom it was sent. Not only were they saved by grace through faith, the same as the Jews, but for the first time they occupied a place of equal privilege with them in the church. They were in no way inferior as far as their standing before God was concerned. And they were destined to be enthroned with Christ as His body and His bride, sharing the glory of His universal reign.

1

I. Introduction to the Letter (1:1-2)

    A. Author (v. 1): *Paul*

    B. Authority (v. 1): *an apostle of Christ Jesus* (RV)

    C. Source of Authority (v. 1): *by the will of God*

    D. Addressees (v. 1): *to the saints which are at Ephesus, and to the faithful in Christ Jesus*

    E. Greeting (v. 2): *Grace to you and peace from God our Father and the Lord Jesus Christ* (RV)

1:1 The name Paul means "small." Although physically he may have fitted this description, spiritually his influence was enormous. He introduces himself as "an apostle of Christ Jesus" (RV). This means that he was commissioned by the ascended Lord to perform a special mission. That mission, of course, was to preach the gospel to the Gentiles and to teach the great truth concerning the church (3:8-9). Since this epistle deals with the subject of the church, and since this truth was first revealed to the apostles and prophets (3:5), it is fitting that Paul should introduce himself as an apostle. It was not a mark of pride for him to do so; rather it was an explanation of how he could speak with authority on the subject.

The source of his authority is expressed in the words "by the will of God." Paul did not choose this work as an occupation. And no men appointed him to it. It was a divine call from beginning to end (Gal. 1:1).

The letter is addressed "to the saints which are at Ephesus, and to the faithful in Christ Jesus." Saints are people who

11

have been separated to God from the world. It is a name which is applied in the New Testament to all born-again believers. Basically the word refers to a believer's position in Christ rather than to what he is in himself. In Christ all believers are saints, even though in themselves they are not always saintly. For instance, Paul addressed the Corinthians as saints (1 Cor. 1:2), even though it is clear from what follows that they were not all living holy lives. Yet God's will is that our practice should correspond to our position: saints should be saintly.

(4) "And to the faithful in Christ Jesus." The word "faithful" means "believing ones" and is thus a description of all true Christians. Of course, believers should also be faithful in the sense that they are reliable and trustworthy. But the primary thought here is that they had acknowledged Christ Jesus to be their only Lord and Savior.

Two of the oldest manuscripts omit the words "at Ephesus." Most Bible scholars think that this was a circular letter, written to be read by local gatherings of Christians in several different places. This is probably true. But few commentaries deny that the assembly at Ephesus was one to which it was sent. Fortunately the question affects neither the authenticity of the letter nor its value for us.

1:2   Next comes the apostle's greeting to the saints. Every word is loaded with spiritual significance—unlike many of the empty greetings we use today.

(5)   Grace, first of all, means divine assistance for daily living! Paul's readers had already been saved by the grace of God, His undeserved favor to the lost. But now they needed strength from God to face the problems, trials and sorrows of life. That is what the apostle wishes for them here.

(6)   Peace means a spirit at rest in all the changing circumstances of life. The saints had already experienced peace with God when they were converted. But day by day they needed the peace of God, that is, the calm, settled repose that is independent of circumstances and that results from taking everything to God in prayer (Phil. 4:6-7).

It is worth noticing that grace comes first, then peace. This is always the order. Only after grace has dealt with the sin question can peace be known. And only through the undeserved strength which God gives from day to day can the believer experience peace, perfect peace, in all the changing moods of life.

"Grace" (Greek: *charis*) was the characteristic Greek way of saying hello. The Jews used the word "peace" (Hebrew: *shalom*). Put them together and we have, in miniature, the gospel for the whole world. And more than that, when we unite them, we have the truth of the New Testament church which Paul expounds so fully in this epistle—Jew and Gentile formed into one body in Christ.

Grace and peace come from God our Father and the Lord Jesus Christ. Paul did not hesitate to put the Lord Jesus on the same level as God the Father; he honored the Son even as he honored the Father. So should we (John 5:23).

Let us not overlook the marvelous conjunction of the words "God our Father." The name God taken by itself might convey the impression of One who is infinitely high and unapproachable. The name Father, on the other hand, speaks of One who is intimately near and accessible. Join the two by the pronoun "our" and we have the staggering truth that the high and lofty One who inhabits eternity is the loving Father of everyone who has been born again through faith in the Lord Jesus.

The full title of our Savior is Lord Jesus Christ. As Lord, He is our absolute Master with full rights to all that we are and have. As Jesus, He is our Savior from sin. As Christ, He is our divinely anointed Prophet, Priest and King. How much His name unfolds to every listening ear!

II. Paul's Praise to God for the Blessings of Grace (1:3-14)

    A. The Blessed One (v. 3): *Blessed be the God and Father of our Lord Jesus Christ*

    B. The Bestower of Blessings (v. 3): *who hath blessed us*

C. The Blessings (v. 3)

    1. Their quantity: *with ALL . . . blessings*
    2. Their quality: *with all SPIRITUAL blessings*
    3. Their locality: *in heavenly places*
    4. Their instrumentality: *in Christ*

D. The Sublime Sweep of God's Eternal Plan for His People (vv. 4-14)

    1. Election (v. 4): *According as he hath chosen us*
      a. Position: *in him*
      b. Time: *before the foundation of the world*
      c. Purpose: *that we should be holy and without blame before Him in love*

    2. Predestination (vv. 5-6): *He destined us*
      a. Wonderful affection (v. 5): *in love*
      b. Glorious adoption (v. 5): *to be his sons*
      c. Prerequisite redemption (v. 5): *through Jesus Christ*
      d. Sovereign motivation (v. 5): *according to the purpose of his will* (RSV)
      e. Eternal adoration (v. 6): *to the praise of his glorious grace*
        1) The terms of His grace: *which he freely bestowed*
        2) The recipients of His grace: *on us*
        3) The channel of His grace: *in the Beloved* (RSV)

    3. Redemption (v. 7)
      a. The Redeemer: *In him [Christ]*
      b. The redeemed: *we have redemption*
      c. The ransom price: *through his blood*
      d. The resulting remission: *the forgiveness of our trespasses*
      e. The richness of remission: *according to the riches of His grace* (RSV)

    4. Wisdom and insight in the mystery of His will (vv. 8-14)
      a. Wisdom and intelligence abundantly provided (v. 8): *Wherein* (that is, in grace) *he hath abounded toward us in all wisdom and prudence*

b. The mystery of His will made known (vv. 9-10): *Having made known unto us the mystery of his will*

1) Its origin (v. 9): *according to his* (God's) *good pleasure*
2) Its principal Subject (v. 9): *which he set forth in Christ* (RSV)
3) Its appointed time (v. 10): *unto a dispensation of the fulness of the times* (RV)
4) Its program (v. 10): *that he might gather together in one all things in Christ*
5) Its inclusiveness (v. 10): *[things] both which are in heaven, and which are on earth; even in him*

c. The mystery in relation to Jewish believers (vv. 11-12)

1) Their title to a share (v. 11): *In whom* (Christ)
2) Their possession of a share (v. 11): *we have obtained an inheritance [or], we were made a heritage* (RV)
3) Their foreordination to a share (vv. 11-12): *being predestinated*
   a) Its sovereign source (v. 11): *according to the purpose of him who worketh all things after the counsel of his own will*
   b) Its positive purpose (v. 12): *That we should be to the praise of his glory*
   c) Its privileged possessors (v. 12): *we . . . who first trusted in Christ*

d. The mystery in relation to Gentile believers (v. 13)

1) Their participation by faith: *In whom ye also trusted*
   a) They heard: *after that ye heard the word of truth, the gospel of your salvation*
   b) They believed: *in whom, having also believed* (RV)
   c) They were sealed: *ye were sealed with that Holy Spirit of promise*

     e. The mystery in relation to both Jewish and Gentile believers (v. 14)
1) The pledge: *Which [Holy Spirit] is the earnest of our inheritance*
2) The realization: *unto the redemption of God's own possession* (RV)
3) The result: *unto the praise of his glory*

1:3 Following his brief salutation, the apostle lifts his voice in a magnificent hymn of praise, soaring into some of the sublimest heights of New Testament worship. Here we have the overflow of a heart that adores God for the blessings of grace. In these verses (3-14), Paul traces God's activity in salvation from eternity past through time and on into eternity future. And this necessarily involves a discussion of the mystery of God's will—believing Jews and Gentiles as co-sharers of the glorious inheritance.

He begins by calling on all who know God to bless Him, that is, to bring joy to His heart by praise and worshiping love. This blessed One is the God and Father of our Lord Jesus Christ. At certain times Jesus addressed God as God (Matt. 27:46). At other times He spoke of Him as Father (John 10:30).

The blessed One is also the Blesser. We bless Him by praising Him. He blesses us, and makes us glad by showering us with the riches of His grace.

He has blessed us with all spiritual blessings in heavenly places in Christ. Here is a pyramid of grace:

blessings

spiritual blessings

all   spiritual   blessings

all spiritual blessings in heavenly places

all spiritual blessings in heavenly places in Christ

Notice, first of all, how unstinted are His heart and hand—*all* spiritual blessings. Notice, too, that these are *spiritual* blessings. The simplest way to explain this is to contrast them with the blessings of Israel under the law. In the Old Testament, a faithful, obedient Jew was rewarded with long life, a large family, abundant crops and protection from his enemies (Deut. 28:2-8). The blessings of Christianity, in contrast, are spiritual, that is, they deal with treasures that are nonmaterial, invisible and imperishable. It is true that the Old Testament saints also enjoyed some spiritual blessings, but as we shall see, the Christian today enjoys blessings that were unknown in previous times.

Our blessings are *in heavenly places,* or *"in the heavenlies"* (RV). Instead of being material blessings in earthly places, they are spiritual blessings *in heavenly places.* The expression "in heavenly places" is used five times in this epistle:

1:3	The sphere of our spiritual blessings
1:20	The scene of Christ's present enthronement
2:6	The scene of our present enthronement in Christ
3:10	The locale from which angels witness God's wisdom exhibited in the church
6:12 (RV)	The region which is the source of our present conflict with evil spirits

When we put these passages together, we have a truly scriptural definition of the heavenly places. They are "the realm of the believer's position and experience as a result of his being united to Christ by the baptism of the Spirit" (Unger).

All spiritual blessings are *in Christ.* It was He who procured them for us through His finished work at Calvary. Now they are available through Him. Everything that God has for the believer is in the Lord Jesus. In order to receive the blessings, we must be united to Christ by faith. The moment a man is *in Christ,* he becomes the possessor of them all. "To be in Christ, which is the portion of all who are saved, is to partake of all that Christ has done, all that He is, and all that He ever will be" (Chafer).

The phrase *in Christ* is one of the key expressions of this epistle. There are two closely related lines of truth in the New Testament—the truth of the believer's position and the truth of his practice.

First, the believer's position. Everyone in the world is either "in Adam" or "in Christ." Those who are "in Adam" are in their sins and therefore condemned before God. There is nothing they can do in themselves to please God or to gain His favor. They have no claim upon God, and if they were to receive what they deserve, they would perish eternally.

When a person is converted, God no longer looks upon him as a condemned child of Adam. Rather He sees him as being in Christ, and He accepts him on that basis. It is important to see this. The believing sinner is not accepted because of what he is in himself, but because he is in Christ. When he is in Christ, he stands before God clothed in all the acceptability of Christ Himself. And he will enjoy God's favor and acceptance as long as Christ does, namely, forever.

The believer's position, then, is what he is in Christ. But there is another side to the picture—the believer's practice. This is what he is in himself. His position is perfect, but his practice is imperfect. Now God's will is that his practice should increasingly correspond to his position. It never will do so perfectly until he is in heaven. But the process of sanctification, growth and increasing Christlikeness should be going on continually here on earth.

When we understand the difference between the believer's standing and his state, it enables us to reconcile such seemingly opposite verses as the following:

Believers are perfect (Heb. 10:4)	Believers should be perfect (Matt. 5:48)
Believers are dead to sin (Rom. 6:2)	Believers should reckon themselves dead to sin (Rom. 6:11)
Believers are a holy nation (I Peter 2:9)	Believers should be holy (I Peter 1:15)

The first column deals with position, the second with practice.

Now to get back to Paul's letter to the Ephesians, the epistle is divided into two main parts:

Chapters 1–3: Our position—what we are in Christ.
Chapters 4–6: Our practice—what we should be in ourselves.

The first half has to do with doctrine, the second half with duty. In the first three chapters, our position is often described by such phrases as "in Christ," "in Christ Jesus," "in Him," "in whom." In the last three chapters, the phrase "in the Lord" is often used to express the believer's responsibility to Christ as Lord. Someone has said that the first part of the letter pictures the believer in the heavenlies in Christ, whereas the last part views him in the kitchen.

Now we are ready to consider some of the spiritual blessings in heavenly places which are ours in Christ.

1:4 The first is what is commonly known as election, "According as he hath chosen us in him before the foundation of the world, that we should be holy and without blame before him in love."

We notice first the positive fact of election in the words *He hath chosen us.* Then there is the positional aspect of the truth, *in Him;* it is in the person and work of the Lord Jesus that all God's purposes for His people are brought to pass. The time of God's election is indicated by the expression *before the foundation of the world.* And the purpose is *that we should be holy and without blame before Him in love.* This purpose will not be completely realized until we are with Him in heaven (I John 3:2), but the process should be going on continually in our lives down here.

Prayer: "Lord, make me holy now, since this is Your eventual purpose for me. Amen."

The doctrine of election raises serious problems in the human mind, and so we are going to consider more fully what the Bible does and does not teach on this subject.

First, it teaches that God does choose men to salvation (II Thess. 2:13). It addresses believers as those who are elect according to the foreknowledge of God (I Peter 1:2). It teaches that people can know whether they are elect by their response to the gospel; those who hear and believe it are elect (I Thess. 1:4-7).

On the other hand, the Bible never teaches that God chooses men to be lost. The fact that He chooses some to be saved does not imply that He arbitrarily condemns all the rest. He never condemns men who deserve to be saved (there are none), but He does save some who ought to be condemned. When Paul describes the elect, he speaks of them as "vessels of mercy which he had afore prepared unto glory" (Rom. 9:23); but when he turns to the lost, he simply says, "vessels of wrath fitted to destruction" (Rom. 9:22). God prepares vessels of mercy to glory, but He does not fit men to destruction; they do this for themselves by their own unbelief.

The doctrine of election lets God be God. He is sovereign, that is, He can do as He pleases, although He never pleases to do anything that is unjust. If left alone, all men would be lost. Does God have the right to show mercy to some?

But there is another side to the story. The same Bible that teaches sovereign election also teaches human responsibility. No one can use the doctrine of election as an excuse for not being saved. God makes a bona fide offer of salvation to all men everywhere (John 3:16; 3:36; 5:24; Rom. 10:9, 13). Anyone can be saved by repenting of his sins and believing on the Lord Jesus Christ. Therefore, if a person is lost, it is because he chooses to be lost, not because God desires it.

The fact is that the same Bible teaches election and free salvation to all who will receive it. Both doctrines are found in a single verse: "All that the Father giveth me shall come to me; and him that cometh to me I will in no wise cast out" (John 6:37). The first half of the verse speaks of God's sovereign choice; the last half extends the offer of mercy to all.

This poses a difficulty for the human mind. How can God choose some and yet offer salvation freely to all men? Frankly, this is a mystery. But the mystery is on our side, not on God's. The best policy for us is to believe both doctrines because the Bible teaches both. The truth is not found somewhere between election and man's free will, but in both extremes. "Divine sovereignty, human responsibility and the free and universal offer of mercy are all found in Scripture, and though we are unable to harmonize them by our logic, they all ought to have a place in our minds" (Pulpit Commentary).

1:5 The second spiritual blessing from the treasury of God's grace is predestination, or foreordination (RV). Though somewhat related to election, it is not the same. Election pictures God's choice of men to salvation. But predestination is an advance on this: it means that God determined ahead of time that all who would be saved would also be adopted into His family as sons. He could have saved us without making us His sons, but He chose to do both.

Many translations take the last two words of verse 4 and link them with verse 5 as follows: "in love having predestinated us. . . ." This reminds us of the unique affection that prompted God to deal with us so graciously.

We have the fact of our glorious adoption in the phrase "having foreordained us unto adoption as sons" (RV). In the New Testament, adoption means placing a believer in the family of God as a mature, adult son with all the privileges and responsibilities of sonship (Gal. 4:4-7). The spirit of adoption plants within the believer the instinct to address God as Father (Rom. 8:15).

Our adoption as sons is "through Christ" (RV). God could never have brought us into this position of nearness and dearness to Himself as long as we were in our sins. So the Lord Jesus came to earth and by His death, burial and resurrection, He settled the sin question to God's satisfaction. It is the infinite value of His sacrifice on Calvary's cross that provides a righteous basis on which God can adopt us as sons.

And it is all "according to the good pleasure of his will." This is the sovereign motivation behind our predestination. It answers the question "Why did He do it?" Simply because it was His good pleasure. He could not be satisfied until He had surrounded Himself with sons, conformed to the image of His only begotten Son, with Him and like Him forever.

1:6 "To the praise of his glorious grace which he freely bestowed on us in the Beloved" (RSV). As Paul has contemplated the grace of God first of all in electing us and then in predestinating us to be His sons, he punctuates his meditation with this refrain that is at once an exclamation, an explanation and an exhortation.

It is an exclamation—a holy gasp at the transcendent glories of such grace.

It is an explanation that the object and the result of all God's gracious dealings with us is His own glory. Eternal adoration is due to Him for such matchless favor. Notice the terms of His grace—"which he *freely* bestowed." The recipients of His grace—"on *us*." The channel of His grace—"in the *Beloved*."

Finally, it is an exhortation. Paul is saying, "Let us praise Him for His glorious grace." Before we go any farther, let us do it!

> Great God of wonders! All Thy ways
> Display Thine attributes divine;
> But the bright glories of Thy grace
> Above Thine other wonders shine:
> Who is a pard'ning God like Thee?
> Or who has grace so rich and free?

1:7 As we trace the sublime sweep of God's eternal plan for His people, we come next to the fact of redemption. This describes that aspect of the work of Christ by which we are freed from the bondage and guilt of sin and introduced into a life of liberty.

The Lord Jesus is the Redeemer ("*in whom* we have redemption"). We are the redeemed. His blood is the ransom price; nothing less would do.

One of the results of redemption is "the forgiveness of our trespasses" (RV). Forgiveness is not the same as redemption; it is one of its fruits. Christ had to make full satisfaction for our sins before they could be forgiven. This was done at the cross. And now—

> Stern justice can demand no more
> And mercy can dispense her store.

The measure of our forgiveness is given in the words "according to the riches of His grace." If we can measure the riches of God's grace, then we can measure how fully He has forgiven us. His grace is infinite! So is His forgiveness!

1:8 It was in grace that He chose us, predestinated us and redeemed us. But that is not all. In that same grace God has superabounded toward us in all wisdom and prudence. This means that He has graciously shared His plans and purposes with us. His desire is that we should have intelligence and insight into His plans for the church and for the universe. And so He has taken us into His confidence, as it were, and has revealed to us the great goal toward which all history is moving.

1:9 The apostle now explains the particular way in which God has abounded toward us in all wisdom and prudence, namely, by making known to us the mystery of His will. As was mentioned in the Introduction, this is the dominant theme of the epistle—the glorious truth concerning Christ and the church.

It is a mystery, not in the sense that it is mysterious, but that it is a sacred secret previously unknown but now revealed to the saints.

This glorious plan originated in the sovereign will of God, quite apart from any outside influences; it was "according to his good pleasure."

And the grand subject of the plan is the Lord Jesus Christ; this is indicated by the clause "which he set forth in Christ" (RSV).

1:10 Now Paul begins a more detailed explanation of the secret of God's plan, and in this chapter he is thinking particularly of the future aspect of the mystery. Chapters 2 and 3 will add further light on the present aspect of the mystery.

The time which Paul has in view is indicated by the expression, "for the administration of the fulness of times" (JND). We understand this to refer to the millennium when Christ will return to the earth to reign as King of kings and Lord of lords. God has a special economy or plan of administration for the final era of human history on this earth.

This plan is "to head up all things in the Christ" (JND). During the millennial reign, all things in heaven and on earth will be summed up in Christ. The Savior who is now rejected and disowned will then be the preeminent One, the Lord of all, the object of universal worship. This is God's goal—to set up Christ as Head over all things, heavenly and earthly, in the kingdom.

The extent of the dominion of Christ is found in the words "the things in the heavens and the things upon the earth" (JND). "This is a secret never made known before. In the prophet Isaiah, we get a beautiful picture of the millennial earth; but do we ever get the millennial heavens with Christ at their head? Was it ever said by Isaiah that all things in heaven and earth should be headed up in the glorified Man?" (Bellett).

This verse (10) is sometimes used to support the false doctrine of universal salvation. It is twisted to suggest that eventually everything and everyone will be restored and reconciled in Christ. But that is quite foreign to the passage. Paul is speaking about universal dominion, not universal salvation.

1:11 One vital feature of the mystery is that believing Jews and believing Gentiles have their share in this grand program of God. The apostle speaks of the mystery in relation to Jewish believers in verses 11 and 12; in relation to Gentile believers in verse 13; then he combines them both in verse 14.

As for the Christians of Jewish ancestry, Paul writes, "In Christ indeed we have been given our share in the heritage, . . ." (NEB), or as the Revised Version reads, "In whom also we were made a heritage." Their right to a share is not based upon their former national privileges, but solely upon their union with Christ. The inheritance here looks forward to the time when they and all true believers will be manifested to an amazed world as the body of Christ, the bride of the Lamb.

From all eternity, these Jewish Christians were marked out for this place of privilege by the sovereign will of God, "being predestinated according to the purpose of him who worketh all things after the counsel of his own will." The purpose of this predestination was that they should be to the praise of His glory. In other words, they are trophies of the grace of God, exhibiting what He can do with such unlikely raw materials, and thus bringing glory to Him.

1:12 The apostle speaks of himself and other believing Jews as "we . . . who have trusted beforehand in Christ" (FWG). He is thinking of the tiny remnant of Jews who responded to the gospel in the early days of Christianity. The good news was first preached to the Jews. Most of the nation of Israel flatly rejected it. But a handful believed on the Lord Jesus. The apostle was one of that number.

It will be different when the Savior returns to the earth the second time. Then the nation will look on Him whom they pierced and will mourn for Him as for an only Son (Zech. 12:10). "And so all Israel shall be saved: as it is written, There shall come out of Sion the Deliverer, and shall turn away ungodliness from Jacob" (Rom. 11:26).

Paul and his Christian contemporaries of Jewish background trusted in the Messiah before the rest of the nation. That is why he uses the description "we . . . who have trusted beforehand in Christ" (FWG).

Those who "fore-hoped" in the Messiah will reign with Him over the earth. The rest of the nation will be the earthly subjects of His kingdom.

1:13 Now Paul switches from believers who had been born Jews to those who had been born Gentiles; he indicates this by changing from "we" to "ye." Those who have been saved from paganism have a share in the mystery of God's will, as well as converted Jews. And so the apostle here traces the steps by which the Ephesians and other Gentiles had been brought into union with Christ.

They heard the gospel.

They believed in Christ.

They were sealed with the Holy Spirit of promise.

First they heard the word of truth, the gospel of their salvation. Basically, this refers to the good news of salvation through faith in the Lord Jesus. But in a wider sense it includes all the teachings of Christ and of the apostles.

Having heard this message, they made a commitment of themselves to Christ by a decisive act of faith. The Lord Jesus is the true object of faith. Salvation is found in Him alone.

As soon as they believed, they were sealed with the Holy Spirit of promise. This simply means that every true believer receives the Spirit of God as a sign that he belongs to God and that he will be kept safe by God until the time when he receives his glorified body. Just as in legal matters a seal indicates ownership and security, so it does in divine affairs. The indwelling Spirit brands us as God's property (I Cor. 6:19-20), and guarantees our preservation until the day of redemption (Eph. 4:30).

Our seal is called the Holy Spirit of promise. First, He is the *Holy* Spirit; this is what He is in Himself. Then, He is the Spirit of *promise*. He was promised by the Father (Joel 2:28; Acts 1:4), and by the Lord Jesus (John 16:7). In addition, He is the guarantee that all God's promises to the believer will be fulfilled.

In the Authorized Version, verse 13 seems to suggest that the sealing takes place some time after conversion. It says: "In whom also after that ye believed, ye were sealed." But the Revised Version reads, "In whom, having also believed, ye were sealed." The sealing takes place the moment a person becomes God's own child, not sometime later.

Verse 13 rounds out the first of many mentions of the Trinity in this letter.

> God the Father (v. 3)
> God the Son (v. 7)
> God the Spirit (v. 13)

1:14 Again Paul changes his pronouns. He merges the "we" of verses 11 and 12 with the "ye" of verse 13, to form the "our" of verse 14. By this deft literary device, he drops a hint of what he will more fully explain in chapters 2 and 3—the union of believing Jews and believing Gentiles to form a new organism, the church.

The Holy Spirit is the earnest of our inheritance. An earnest is a downpayment, pledging that the full amount will be paid. It is the same in kind as the full payment, but not the same in amount.

As soon as we are saved, the Holy Spirit begins to reveal to us some of the riches that are ours in Christ. He gives us foretastes of the coming glory. But how can we be sure that we will get the full inheritance some day? The Holy Spirit Himself is the earnest.

As the seal, He guarantees that we ourselves will be kept safely for the inheritance. As the earnest, He guarantees that the inheritance will be kept securely for us.

The Spirit is the earnest "unto the redemption of God's own possession" (RV). The earnest looks forward to the full redemption, just as the firstfruits look forward to the complete harvest. The Spirit's role as earnest will cease when God's own possession is redeemed. But what does Paul mean by God's own possession?

1. He may mean our inheritance. All that God possesses is ours through the Lord Jesus; we are heirs of God and joint heirs with Jesus Christ (Rom. 8:17; I Cor. 3:21-23). The universe itself has been defiled through the entrance of sin, and needs to be reconciled and purified (Col. 1:20; Heb. 9:23). When Christ returns to the earth to reign, this groaning creation will be delivered from the bondage of corruption into the glorious liberty of the children of God (Rom. 8:19-22).

2. The expression "God's own possession" may mean the believer's body. Our spirits and souls were redeemed when we first believed, but the redemption of our bodies is still future. The fact that we suffer, grow old and die proves that our bodies have not yet been redeemed. When Christ returns for us (I Thess. 4:13-18), our bodies will be fashioned anew that they might be conformed to the body of His glory (Phil. 3:21). Then they will be fully and forever redeemed (Rom. 8:23).

3. Finally, "God's own possession" may refer to the church (I Peter 2:9, RV, "a people for God's own possession"). In this case, its redemption also looks forward to the rapture when Christ will present the church to Himself a glorious church without spot or wrinkle or any such thing (Eph. 5:27). Some believe that in this view, God's own possession may also include the Old Testament saints.

Whichever view we hold, the ultimate result is the same—"unto the praise of His glory." God's marvelous plan for His people will then have reached a glorious consummation, and He will be the object of continual praise.

Three times in this chapter Paul has reminded us that the intended goal and inevitable result of all God's actions is that He should be magnified and glorified.

> To the praise of the glory of His grace (v. 6)
> That we should be to the praise of His glory (v. 12)
> Unto the praise of His glory (v. 14)

III. Paul's Thanksgiving and Prayers for the Saints (1:15-23)

    A. Thanksgiving for Their Spiritual Condition (vv. 15-16a)

        1. Faith (v. 15): *Wherefore I also, after I heard of your faith in the Lord Jesus*

        2. Love (vv. 15b-16a): *and love unto all the saints, cease not to give thanks for you*

    B. Prayer for Their Spiritual Illumination (vv. 16b-23): *making mention of you in my prayers*

        1. The source of spiritual illumination (v. 17): *that the God of our Lord Jesus Christ, the Father of glory*

2. The channel (v. 17): *may give unto you the spirit of wisdom and revelation*

3. The supreme subject (v. 17): *in the full-knowledge of him* (FWG)

4. The organs of enlightenment (v. 18): *having the eyes of your hearts enlightened* (RSV)

5. The specific areas of knowledge requested (vv. 18-23)
   a. The hope (v. 18): *that ye may know what is the hope of his calling*
   b. The inheritance (v. 18): *and what the riches of the glory of his inheritance in the saints*
   c. The power (v. 19): *And what is the exceeding greatness of his power to us-ward who believe*
      1) Its infinite potential (v. 19): *according to that working of the strength of his might* (RV)
      2) Its greatest manifestation (vv. 20-23): *Which he wrought in Christ*
         a) Resurrection (v. 20): *when he raised him from the dead*
         b) Glorification (v. 20): *and set him at his own right hand in the heavenly places*
         c) Dominion (vv. 21-22a)
            i. Over created beings (v. 21): *Far above all principality, and power, and might, and dominion, and every name that is named, not only in this world (age), but also in that which is to come*
            ii. Over created things (v. 22a): *And hath put all things under his feet*
         d) Association (vv. 22-23): *and gave him to be the head over all things to the church*
            i. His body (v. 23a): *Which is his body*
            ii. His complement (v. 23b): *the fulness of him that filleth all in all*

1:15 In the preceding, record-breaking sentence, extending from verse 3 through verse 14, the apostle has traced the thrilling sweep of God's program from eternity past to eternity future. He has ranged over some of the most awe-inspiring thoughts that can occupy the human mind, thoughts so exalted that Paul now shares with his readers his deep prayer burden for their spiritual enlightenment in such concepts. His great desire for them is that they might appreciate their glorious privileges in Christ and the tremendous power which was required to give Christ to the church as Head over all creation.

The introductory phrase "For this cause . . . ." looks back to all that God has done and will yet do for those who are members of the body of Christ, as described in verses 3-14.

"After I heard of your faith in the Lord Jesus and love unto all the saints." It was when he received this information that Paul was assured that his readers were possessors of the spiritual blessings just described and was driven to prayer for them. Their faith in the Lord Jesus brought the miracle of salvation to their lives. Their love to all the saints demonstrated the transforming reality of their conversion.

We have previously mentioned that many Bible scholars do not think that this letter was written exclusively to the Ephesians. They point to this verse as evidence. Paul speaks here of having heard of the faith of his readers—as if he had never met them. But he had spent at least three years in Ephesus (Acts 20:31). They therefore conclude that the letter was sent to several local congregations, of which Ephesus was only one.

Fortunately the question does not affect the lessons we can learn from the verse. For instance, we see here that the Lord Jesus is presented as the true object of faith: "your faith in the Lord Jesus." We are not told to believe in a creed, in the church, or in Christians. Saving faith is in the risen, exalted Christ at God's right hand.

Another lesson for us is in the expression "your love to *all* the saints." Our love should not be limited to those of our own area of fellowship, but should flow out to all who have been cleansed by the blood of Christ, to all the household of faith.

A third lesson is found in the combination of faith and

love. Some people say they have faith, but it is hard to find any love in their lives. Others profess great love but are quite indifferent to the necessity of faith in Christ. True Christianity combines sound doctrine and sound living.

1:16 The faith and love of the believers impelled the apostle to praise the Lord for them and to pray for them unceasingly. "Thanksgiving is for the foundation already laid, but intercession is for the superstructure going up. Thanksgiving is for past attainments but intercession is for future advancements. Thanksgiving is for the actual in their experience, but intercession is for the possible in God's purpose for them" (Scroggie).

1:17 What a privilege it is for us to have this glimpse into the prayer life of a man of God. In fact, we have two such glimpses in this letter—here and in 3:14-21. Here the prayer is for spiritual illumination; there it is for spiritual strength. Here the prayer is addressed to God; there to the Father. But in every case Paul's prayers were unceasing, specific and appropriate to the current needs of the people.

Here the prayer is addressed to "the God of our Lord Jesus Christ, the Father of glory." The expression "the Father of glory" may mean that God is either:

1. the source or Originator of all glory,
2. the One to whom all glory belongs, or
3. the Father of the Lord Jesus, who is the manifestation of God's glory

The prayer continues that He "may give unto you the spirit of wisdom and revelation in the knowledge of him." The Holy Spirit is the Spirit of wisdom (Isa. 11:2), and of revelation (I Cor. 2:10). But since every believer is indwelt by Him, Paul cannot be praying that his readers might receive the person of the Holy Spirit but rather that they might receive a special measure of illumination from Him.

Revelation deals with the imparting of knowledge; wisdom has to do with the proper use of it in our lives. The apostle is not thinking of knowledge in general but of "the full knowledge of Him" (FWG). He wants the believers to have a deep, spiritual and experimental knowledge of God—a knowledge that cannot be gained by intellectual ability, but only by the gracious ministry of the Spirit.

"These Ephesian Christians had already divine illumination, or they would not have been Christians at all; but Paul prayed that the Divine Spirit who dwelt in them would make their vision clearer, keener, stronger, that the divine power and love and greatness might be revealed to them far more fully. And perhaps in these days in which men are making such rapid discoveries in inferior provinces of thought, discoveries so fascinating and so exciting as to rival in interest, even for Christian men, the manifestation of God in Christ, there is exceptional need for the Church to pray that God would grant it 'a spirit of wisdom and revelation.' If He were to answer that prayer, we would no longer be dazzled by the knowledge which relates to things seen and temporal. It would be outshone by the transcendent glory of things unseen and eternal" (Dale).

1:18 We have seen that the source of spiritual illumination is God; the channel is the Holy Spirit; and the supreme subject is the full knowledge of God. Now we come to the organs of enlightenment: "having the eyes of your hearts enlightened" (RSV).

This figurative expression teaches us that proper understanding of divine realities is not dependent on our having a keen intellect but rather a tender heart. It is a matter of the affections as well as of the mind. God's revelations are given to those who love Him. This opens up wonderful possibilities for every believer because though we may not all have high I.Q.'s, we can all have loving hearts.

Next Paul specifies the three particular areas of divine knowledge which he desires for the saints:

1. the hope of His calling
2. the riches of the glory of His inheritance in the saints
3. the exceeding greatness of His power to usward who believe

"The hope of his calling" points forward to the future; it means that eventual destiny which He had in mind for us when He called us. It includes the fact that we shall be with Christ and like Him forever. We shall be manifested to the universe as sons of God, and shall reign with Him as His spotless bride. We hope for this, not in the sense that there is any doubt about it, but rather because it is that aspect of our salvation which is still future and to which we look forward.

"The riches of the glory of his inheritance in the saints" is the second tremendous vastness for believers to explore. Notice the way in which Paul stacks words upon words in order to produce the effect of immensity and grandeur:

His inheritance

His inheritance in the saints

The glory of His inheritance in the saints

The riches of the glory of His inheritance in the saints

There are two possible ways of understanding this, and both are so meaningful that we dare not choose between them. According to the first, the saints are His inheritance and He looks upon them as a treasure of incomparable worth. In verse 11 (ASV), believers were spoken of as a heritage, and in Titus 2:14 (RV) and I Peter 2:9 (RV), they are described as a people for God's own possession. It is certainly an exhibition of unspeakable grace that vile, unworthy sinners, saved through Christ, could ever occupy such a place in the heart of God that He would speak of them as His inheritance.

The other view is that the inheritance means all that we will inherit. In brief, it means the whole universe put under the reign of Christ, and we, His bride, reigning with Him over it. If we really appreciate the wealth of the glory of all that He has in store for us, it will spoil us for the attractions and pleasures of this world.

1:19   The third petition of Paul for the saints is that they might have a deep appreciation of the power which God engages to bring all this to pass; he calls it "the exceeding greatness of his power to us-ward who believe."

"It is *power*. It is *His* power. It is *great* power; nothing less would suffice. It is *exceeding* great power, beyond the furthest cast of thought" (F. B. Meyer).

This is the power which God used in our redemption, which He uses in our preservation, and which He will yet use in our glorification. "Paul wants to impress the believer with the greatness of the power which is engaged to accomplish for him everything that God has purposed according to His work of election, predestination and sovereign adoption" (Chafer).

To further emphasize the magnitude of this power, the apostle next describes the greatest exhibition of divine power that the world has ever known, namely, the power that raised Christ out from among the dead and enthroned Him at God's right hand. Perhaps we would think that the creation of the universe was the greatest display of God's might. Or God's miraculous deliverance of His people through the Red Sea. But no! The New Testament teaches us that His resurrection and ascension required the greatest outflow of divine energy.

Why was this? It seems that all the hosts of hell were massed to frustrate God's purposes by keeping Christ in the tomb, or by preventing His ascension once He was raised. But God triumphed over every form of opposition. Christ's resurrection and glorification were a shattering defeat for Satan and his hosts, and a glorious spectacle of victorious power.

No one word is sufficient to describe such power. So Paul borrows several from the vocabulary of dynamics in his description of the power which is employed on our behalf: "according to that *working* of the *strength* of His *might* which He *energized* in Christ" when He raised Him from the dead. As someone has said, the words seem to bend under the weight of the idea. It is hardly necessary for us to distinguish between the different words; it is enough to marvel at the immensity of the power and to worship our God for His omnipotence.

1:20 "A marvelous lift was there! From the grave of mortality to the throne of the eternal God, who only has immortality. From the darkness of the tomb to the insufferable light. From this small world to the center and metropolis of the universe. Open the compasses of your faith to measure this measureless abyss. Then marvel at the power which bore your Lord across it" (Meyer).

As far as the Scriptures are concerned, the resurrection of Christ was the first such event in human history (I Cor. 15:23). Others had been raised from the dead, but they died again. The Lord Jesus was the first to rise in the power of an endless life.

Following Christ's resurrection and ascension, God made Him to sit at His right hand in heavenly places. The right hand of God signifies the place of privilege (Heb. 1:13), of power (Matt. 26:64), of distinction (Heb. 1:3), of delight (Ps. 16:11), and of dominion (I Peter 3:22).

The location is further described as "in the heavenly places." This indicates that the phrase "the heavenlies" (RV) includes the dwelling place of God. That is where the Lord Jesus is today in a literal body of flesh and bones, a glorified body no longer capable of dying. Where He is, we soon shall be.

1:21 The glorification of our Savior is further described as "far above all principality, and power, and might, and dominion, and every name that is named, not only in this world [age], but also in that which is to come." This simply means that the Lord Jesus is superior to every ruler or authority, human or angelic, now or forever.

In the heavenlies there are different ranks of angelic beings, some evil and some good. They have different degrees of power. Some, for instance, might correspond to our human offices of president, governor, mayor or ward alderman.

No matter how great their rule, authority, power and dominion might be, Christ is far above them.

And this is true not only in the age in which we live but also in the coming age, that is, the literal thousand-year reign of Christ on earth. He will then be King over all kings and Lord over all lords. He will be exalted above all created beings; no exception can be named.

1:22   In addition, God has put all created *things* under His feet. This signifies universal dominion, not only over men and angels, but over all the rest of His creation, animate and inanimate.

The writer of the epistle to the Hebrews reminds us that at the present time we do not see all things put under Him (Heb. 2:8). That is true. Though universal dominion belongs to Christ, He does not exercise it as yet. Men, for instance, still rebel against Him, and deny Him or resist Him. But God has decreed that His Son will yet wield the scepter of universal dominion, and it is as certain as if it were a present reality.

What follows is almost incredible. This One whose nail-scarred hand will exercise sovereign authority over all the universe—God has given this glorious One to the church! Here Paul makes a startling revelation concerning the mystery of God's will; step by step he has been leading up to this climactic announcement. With graphic skill he has been describing the resurrection, glorification and dominion of Christ. While our hearts are still awestruck at the contemplation of this all-glorious Lord, the apostle says, "It is in His capacity as Head over all things that Christ has been given to the Church."

If we read this verse carelessly, we might understand it to say that Christ is the Head of the church. While that is true enough, the verse says a lot more. It says that the church is closely associated with Him who has been given universal sway.

In verse 21 we learned that Christ is far above every *creature* in heaven and on earth, in this age and in the coming age. In the first part of verse 22 we learned that all *things* as well as all created beings are in subjection under His feet. Now we learn that the unique calling of the church is to be associated with Him in His boundless dominion. The church will share His rule. All the rest of creation will be under His rule.

1:23 In this final verse of the chapter, we learn how close is the relationship between Christ and the church. Two figures are given:

1. The church is His body.
2. It is the fullness of Him who fills all in all.

No relationship could be closer than that of the head and the body. They are one in vital union and indwelt by one spirit. The church is a company of people called out from the world between Pentecost and the rapture, saved by marvelous grace, and given the unique privilege of being the body of Christ. No other group of believers in any age ever has had or will have this distinction.

The second description of the church is "the fulness of Him that filleth all in all." This simply means that the church is the complement of Christ, who is everywhere at one and the same time. A complement is that which fills up or completes. It implies two things which when brought together constitute a whole. Just as a body is the complement of the head, so the church is the complement of Christ.

But lest anyone should think that this implies any imperfection or incompleteness in Christ, the apostle quickly adds, "the fulness of him that filleth all in all." Far from His needing anything to fill up any lack of completeness, the Lord Jesus is Himself the One who fills all in all, who permeates the universe, and supplies it with all that it needs.

Admittedly, this is too much for us to understand. We can only admire the infinite mind and plan of God while admitting our own inability to comprehend it.

2

IV. God's Power Manifest in the Salvation of Gentiles and Jews (2:1-10)

A. The Sinful Condition of the Unconverted Gentiles (vv. 1-2)

1. Dead (v. 1): *And you . . . who were dead in trespasses and sins*
2. Depraved (v. 2): *Wherein in time past ye walked according to the course of this world*
3. Diabolical (v. 2): *according to the prince of the power of the air*
4. Disobedient (v. 2): *of the spirit who is now working in the sons of disobedience:* (NASB)

B. The Similar Condition of the Unconverted Jews (v. 3)

1. Carnal: *Among whom also we all had our conversation in times past in the lusts of our flesh*
2. Corrupt: *fulfilling the desires of the flesh and of the mind*
3. Condemned: *and were by nature the children of wrath, even as others*

C. The Stupendous Change That Has Occurred (vv. 4-7)

1. Its Author (v. 4): *But God, . . .*
2. His character (v. 4): *who is rich in mercy*
3. The reason for His intervention (v. 4): *for his great love wherewith he loved us*
4. Our unlovely condition (v. 5): *Even when we were dead in trespasses* (FWG)

5. His mighty accomplishments (vv. 5b-7)
   a. Quickened (v. 5b): *hath quickened us*
      1) Explanation: *together with Christ*
      2) Exclamation: *by grace ye are saved*
   b. Raised (v. 6a): *And hath raised us up together*
   c. Seated (v. 6b): *and made us sit together*
      1) Our privileged place: *in heavenly places*
      2) Our personal position: *in Christ Jesus*
6. The ultimate purpose (v. 7)
   a. Time: *That in the ages to come*
   b. Action: *he [God] might shew*
   c. Display: *the exceeding riches of his grace in his kindness toward us through Christ Jesus*

D. The Simple Plan of Salvation (vv. 8-10)

1. Its origin (v. 8): *For by grace*
2. Its present certainty (v. 8): *ye are saved* (JND)
3. Its manner of reception (v. 8): *through faith*
4. Its impossibility of self-attainment (v. 8): *and that not of yourselves*
5. Its essential character (v. 8): *it is the gift of God*
6. Its positive exclusion (v. 9): *Not of works*
7. Its reason for this exclusion (v. 9): *lest any man should boast*
8. Its result (v. 10): *For we are his workmanship*
9. Its new creation (v. 10): *created in Christ Jesus*
10. Its goal (v. 10): *unto good works*
11. Its prepared plan for each life (v. 10): *which God hath afore prepared that we should walk in them* (RV)

2:1 We must not let the chapter-break rob us of the vital connection between the latter part of chapter 1 and the verses that follow. There we watched the mighty power of God as it raised Christ from the grave and crowned Him with glory and honor. Now we see how that same power has worked in our own lives, raising us from spiritual death and seating us in Christ in the heavenlies.

This passage resembles the first chapter of Genesis.   In each we have:

1. a scene of desolation, chaos and ruin (Gen. 1:2*a*; Eph. 2:1-3)
2. the introduction of divine power (Gen. 1:2*b*; Eph. 2:4)
3. the creation of new life (Gen. 1:3-31; Eph. 2:5-22)

When Ephesians 2 opens, we are spiritual corpses in death valley. When it closes, we are not only seated in Christ in the heavenlies; we form a habitation of God through the Spirit. In between we have the mighty miracle that brought about this remarkable transformation.

The first ten verses describe God's power in the salvation of Gentiles and of Jews. No Cinderella ever advanced from such rags to such riches!

In verses 1 and 2, Paul reminds his Gentile readers that before their conversion, they were dead, depraved, diabolical and disobedient. They were spiritually dead as a result of their trespasses and sins. This means that they were lifeless toward God. They had no vital contact with Him. They lived as if He did not exist.

The cause of death was "trespasses and sins." Sin is any form of wrongdoing, whether consciously committed or not. It is any thought, word or deed which falls short of God's perfection. Trespasses are sins which are committed in open violation of a known law. In a wider sense, they may also include any form of false steps or blunders.

2:2   The Ephesians had been depraved as well as dead. They "walked according to the course of this world." They conformed to the spirit of this age. They indulged in the sins of the times. The world has a mold into which it pours its devotees. It is a mold of deceit, immorality, ungodliness, selfishness, violence and rebellion. In a word, it is a mold of depravity. That is what the Ephesians had been like.

Not only so, their behavior was diabolical. They followed the example of the devil, "the prince of the power of the air." They were led around by the chief ruler of evil spirits whose realm is the atmosphere. They were willingly obedient to the god of this age. This explains why the unconverted often stoop to vile forms of behavior lower than that of animals.

Finally, they were disobedient, walking according to "the spirit that now worketh in the sons of disobedience" (ASV). All unsaved people are sons of disobedience in the sense that they are characterized by disobedience to God. They are energized by Satan, and are therefore disposed to defy, dishonor and disobey the Lord.

2:3 Paul's switch of the personal pronoun from *you* to *we* indicates that he is now speaking primarily of Jewish believers (though what he says is also true of everyone before conversion). Three words describe their status: carnal, corrupt and condemned.

"Among whom also we all had our conversation in times past in the lusts of our flesh." It was among the sons of disobedience that Paul and his fellow Christians also walked prior to their new birth. Their life was *carnal*, concerned only with the gratification of fleshly desires and appetites. The apostle himself had lived an outwardly moral life on the whole, but now he realized how self-centered it was. And what he was in himself was a lot worse than anything he had ever done.

The unconverted Jews were also *corrupt* "fulfilling the desires of the flesh and of the mind." This indicates an abandonment to every natural desire. Desires of the flesh and mind may range all the way from legitimate appetites to various forms of immorality and perversion; here the emphasis is probably on the grosser sins. And notice, Paul refers to sins of thought as well as to sinful acts. "It is as ruinous to indulge the desires of the *mind* as those of the *flesh*. By the marvelous gift of imagination we may indulge unholy fancies, and throw the reins on the neck of the steeds of passion— always stopping short of the act. No human eye follows the soul when it goes forth to dance with satyrs or to thread the labyrinthine maze of the islands of desire. It goes and returns unsuspected by the nearest. Its credit for snow-white purity is not forfeited. It is still permitted to watch among the virgins for the Bridegroom's advent. But if this practice is unjudged and unconfessed, it marks the offender a son of disobedience and a child of wrath" (F. B. Meyer).

That is Paul's final description of the unsaved Jews: they were by nature "children of wrath, even as others." This means that they had a natural predisposition to anger, malice, bitterness, and hot temper. They shared this with the rest of mankind.

Of course, it is also true that they are under the wrath of God. They are appointed to death and to judgment. Notice that man's three enemies are mentioned in verses 2 and 3:

1. the world (v. 2)
2. the devil (v. 2)
3. the flesh (v. 3)

2:4   Here the words *"But God, . . ."* form one of the most significant, eloquent and inspiring transitions in all literature. They indicate that a stupendous change has taken place. It is a change from the doom and despair of the valley of death to unspeakable delights of the kingdom of the Son of God's love.

The Author of the change is God Himself. No one else could have done it, and no one else would have done it.

One characteristic of this blessed One is that He is rich in mercy. He shows mercy to us by not treating us the way we deserve to be treated (Ps. 103:10). And He is rich in mercy. "Though it has been expended by Him for six millennia, and myriads and myriads have been partakers of it, it is still an unexhausted mine of wealth" (Eadie).

The reason for His intervention is given in the words: "for his great love wherewith he loved us." His love is great because He is its source. Just as the greatness of a giver casts an aura of greatness on his gift, so the surpassing excellence of God adds superlative luster to His love. It is greater to be loved by the mighty Sovereign of the universe, for instance, than by a fellow human being.

God's love is great because of the price which He paid. Love sent the Lord Jesus, God's only begotten Son, to die for us in agony at Calvary.

God's love is great because of the unsearchable riches it showers on its objects.

2:5 And God's love is great because of the extreme unworthiness and unloveliness of the persons loved. We were dead through trespasses. We were enemies of God. We were destitute and degraded. He loved us in spite of it all.

As a result of God's love for us, and as a result of the redeeming work of Christ, we have been:

1. quickened with Christ
2. raised up with Him
3. seated in Him

These expressions describe our spiritual position as a result of our union with Him. He acted as our Representative— not only *for* us, but *as* us. Therefore when He died, we died. When He was buried, we were buried.

When He was quickened, raised and seated in the heavenlies, so were we. All the benefits of His sacrificial work are enjoyed by us because of our link with Him.

To be "quickened together with" Him means that converted Jews and converted Gentiles are now associated with Him in newness of life. The same power that gave Him resurrection life has given it to us also.

The marvel of this causes Paul to interrupt his train of thought and to exclaim, "By grace have ye been saved" (RV). He is overwhelmed by the fathomless favor which God has shown to those who deserved the very opposite. That is grace!

We have already mentioned that mercy means we do not get the punishment we deserve. Grace means we get the salvation we do not deserve. We get it as a gift, not as some-

thing we earn. And it comes from One who was not compelled to give it. "It is a voluntary exercise of love for which
He is under no obligation. What constituted the glory of
grace is that it is an utterly unfettered, unconstrained exercise of the love of God toward poor sinners" (Dr. A. T.
Pierson).

2:6 Not only have we been quickened with Christ; we
have also been raised with Him. Just as death and judgment
are behind Him, they are behind us also. We stand on the
resurrection side of the tomb. This is our glorious position
as a result of our union with Him. And because it is true
of us positionally, we should live as those who are alive from
the dead.

Another aspect of our position is that we are seated in Him
in the heavenlies in Christ. By our union with Him, we are
seen as already delivered from this present evil world and
seated in Christ in glory. This is how God sees us. If we
appropriate it by faith, it will change the character of our
lives. We will no longer be earthbound, occupied with the
trivial and the transient. We will seek those things which
are above, where Christ is seated at the right hand of God.

The key to verses 5 and 6 is the phrase "in Christ Jesus."
It is in Him that we have been quickened, raised and seated.
He is our Representative; therefore, His triumphs are ours
and His position is ours. "Amazing thought! That a Mary
Magdalene and a crucified thief should be the companions
in glory of the Son of God" (George Williams).

2:7 This miracle of transforming grace will be the subject of eternal revelation. Throughout the endless ages God
will be unveiling to the heavenly throng what it cost Him to
send His Son to this jungle of sin, and what it cost the Lord
Jesus to bear our sins at the cross. It is a subject that will
never be exhausted. Again Paul builds words upon words to
describe something of its immensity:

His kindness toward us

His grace in His kindness toward us

The riches of His grace in His kindness toward us

The exceeding riches of His grace in His kindness toward us

Now it follows that if God will be disclosing this throughout eternity, then we will be learning forever and ever. Heaven will be our school. God will be the Teacher. His grace will be the subject. We will be the students. And the school term will be eternity.

This should deliver us from the idea that we will know everything when we get to heaven. Only God knows everything and we will never be equal with Him.*

It also raises the interesting question: How much will we know when we get to heaven? And it suggests the possibility that we can prepare for the heavenly university by majoring in the Bible right now.

2:8 The next three verses present as clear a statement of the simple plan of salvation as we can find in the Bible.

It all originates with the grace of God; He takes the initiative in providing it. Salvation is given to those who are utterly unworthy of it, on the basis of the person and work of the Lord Jesus Christ.

It is given as a present possession. Those who are saved can know it. Writing to the Ephesians, Paul said, "You have been saved." He knew it, and they knew it.

The way we receive the gift of eternal life is through faith. Faith means that man takes his place as a lost, guilty sinner, and receives the Lord Jesus as his only hope of salvation. True saving faith is the commitment of a person to a Person.

Any idea that man can earn or deserve salvation is forever exploded by the words "and that not of yourselves." Dead

*First Corinthians 13:12 and I John 3:2 are sometimes used to prove that we will be omniscient in heaven. However, the first deals only with recognition of one another in heaven and the second with moral and physical likeness to Christ.

people can *do* nothing and sinners *deserve* nothing but punishment.

"It is the gift of God." A gift, of course, is a free and unconditional present. That is the only basis on which God offers salvation.

Some people have mistakenly understood the statement "It is the gift of God" to refer to faith. Building on this false premise, they go on to argue that a man cannot believe unless God gives him faith. Therefore, it is all dependent on God, and there is nothing a man can do about it. This is certainly not Bible doctrine.

The gift of God in this verse is *salvation by grace through faith.* It is offered freely to all men everywhere.

2:9 It is not of works, that is, it is not something a person can earn through supposedly meritorious deeds. It cannot be earned, for instance, by:

> Confirmation
> Baptism
> Church membership
> Church attendance
> Holy Communion
> Trying to keep the Ten Commandments
> Living by the Sermon on the Mount
> Giving to charity
> Being a good neighbor
> Living a moral, respectable life

Man is not saved by works. And he is not saved by faith plus works. He is saved by faith alone. The minute you add works of any kind or in any amount as a means of gaining eternal life, salvation would no longer be by grace (Rom. 11:6).

The reason that works are positively excluded is to prevent human boasting.

If a man could be saved by his works, then he would have reason to boast before God. This is impossible (Rom. 3:27).

If a man could be saved by his own good works, then the death of Christ was unnecessary (Gal. 2:21). But we know that the reason He died was because there was no other way by which guilty sinners could be saved.

If a man could be saved by his own good works, then he would be his own savior, and could worship himself. But this would be idolatry and God forbids it (Exodus 20:3).

Even if a man could be saved by faith in Christ plus his own good works, you would have the impossible situation of two saviors—Jesus and the sinner. Christ would then have to share the glory of saviorhood with another, and this He will not do (Isa. 42:8).

Finally, if man could contribute to his salvation by works, then God would owe it to him. This, too, is impossible. God cannot be indebted to anyone (Rom. 11:35).

In contrast to works, faith excludes boasting (Rom. 3:27), because it is nonmeritorious. Though a man has no reason to be proud that he has trusted the Lord, faith in Him is the most sane, rational, sensible thing a person can do. To trust one's Creator and Redeemer is only logical and reasonable. If we cannot trust Him, whom can we trust?

2:10 The result of salvation is that we are *His* workmanship—the handiwork of God, not of ourselves. A born-again believer is a masterpiece of God. When we think of the raw materials He has to work with, His achievement is all the more remarkable.

Indeed, this masterpiece is nothing less than a new creation through union with Christ, for "if any man be in Christ, he is a new creature: old things are passed away; behold, all things are become new" (II Cor. 5:17).

And the object of this new creation is found in the phrase "unto good works." While it is true that we are not saved *by* good works, it is equally true that we are saved *unto* good works. Good works are not the *root* but the *fruit*. We do not work *in order to be saved*, but *because we are saved*.

This is the aspect of the truth that is emphasized in James 2:14-26. When James says that "faith without works is dead," he does not mean that we are saved by faith plus works, but by the kind of faith that results in a life of good works. Works prove the reality of our faith.

Paul heartily agrees; he says, "we are his workmanship, created in Christ Jesus unto good works."

God's order then is this:

Faith——Salvation——Good Works——Reward

Faith leads to salvation. Salvation results in good works. Good works will be rewarded by Him.

But the question arises: What kind of good works am I expected to do? Paul answers, "Good works, which God prepared beforehand that we should walk in them" (RSV). In other words, God has a blueprint for every life. Before our conversion, He mapped out a spiritual career for us. Our responsibility is to find His will for us and then to obey it. It has been well said that we do not have to work out a plan for our lives, but only to receive the plan which He has drawn up for us. This delivers us from fret and from frenzy, and insures that our lives will be of maximum glory to Him, of most blessing to others, and of greatest reward to ourselves.

In order to find out the good works which He has planned for our individual lives, we should:

1. confess and forsake sin as soon as we are conscious of it in our lives
2. be continually and unconditionally yielded to Him
3. study the Word of God to discern His will, and then do whatever He tells us to do
4. spend time in prayer each day
5. seize opportunities of service as they arise
6. cultivate the fellowship and counsel of other Christians

God prepares us for good works. He prepares good works for us to perform. Then He rewards us when we perform them. Such is His grace!

V. The Union of Believing Jews and Gentiles in Christ (2:11-22)

   A. The Past Status of Paul's Readers Nationally (vv. 11-12): *Wherefore remember, that ye being in time past Gentiles in the flesh*

      1. Despised (v. 11): *who are called Uncircumcision by that which is called the Circumcision in the flesh made by hands*

      2. Christless (v. 12): *That at that time ye were without Christ*

      3. Aliens (v. 12): *being aliens from the commonwealth of Israel*

      4. Strangers (v. 12): *and strangers from the covenants of promise*

      5. Hopeless (v. 12): *having no hope*

      6. Pagan (v. 12): *and without God in the world*

   B. The New Status of Believing Gentiles (v. 13)

      1. The new relationship: *But now in Christ Jesus*

      2. The new nearness: *ye who sometimes were far off are made nigh*

      3. The cost of effecting the change: *by the blood of Christ*

   C. Believing Jews and Gentiles Now Made One in Christ (vv. 14-18)

      1. The basis of union (v. 14): *For he is our peace*

      2. The scope of Christ's work (vv. 14b-18)

         a. Union (v. 14): *who hath made both one*

         b. Demolition (v. 14): *and hath broken down the middle wall of partition between us*

         c. Abolition (v. 15): *Having abolished in his flesh the enmity, even the law of commandments contained in ordinances*

         d. Creation (v. 15): *for to make in himself of twain one new man*

         e. Pacification (v. 15): *so making peace*

         f. Reconciliation (v. 16): *And that he might reconcile both unto God in one body*

            1) The means: *by the cross*

            2) The method: *having slain the enmity thereby*

      g. Proclamation (v. 17): *And he came and preached peace to you who were far off and peace to those who were near* (RSV)

      h. Admission (v. 18)

         1) The Mediator: *For through him [Christ]*

         2) The participants: *we both [believing Jews and Gentiles]*

         3) The privilege: *have access*

         4) The Helper: *by one Spirit*

         5) The One we approach: *unto the Father*

D. The Privileges of Believing Gentiles (vv. 19-22)

    1. No longer outcasts (v. 19): *Now therefore ye are no more strangers and foreigners*

    2. Now fellow citizens (v. 19): *but fellowcitizens with the saints*

    3. Now family members (v. 19): *and of the household of God*

    4. Now built into a holy temple (vv. 20-22)

      a. Foundation (v. 20): *And are built upon the foundation of the apostles and prophets*

      b. Chief cornerstone (v. 20): *Jesus Christ himself being the chief corner stone*

      c. Source of growth (v. 21): *In whom [Christ]*

      d. Unity and symmetry (v. 21): *all the building fitly framed together*

      e. Unique feature (v. 21): *groweth*

      f. Type of building (v. 21): *unto an holy temple*

      g. Its source of holiness (v. 21): *in the Lord:*

      h. Equal place of believing Gentiles in the building program (v. 22): *In whom ye also are builded together*

      i. Purpose of the temple (v. 22): *for an habitation of God*

      j. The One by whom He indwells the temple (v. 22): *in the Spirit* (RSV)

In the first half of chapter 2 we followed Paul as he traced the salvation of individual Gentiles and Jews. Now he advances to the abolition of their former national differences, to their union in Christ and to their formation into the church, a holy temple in the Lord.

2:11 In verses 11 and 12, the apostle reminds his readers that prior to their conversion they were Gentiles by birth and therefore outcasts as far as the Jews were concerned.

First, they were despised. This is indicated by the fact that the Jews called them "uncircumcision." This meant, of course, that the Gentiles did not have the surgical sign in their flesh that marked the Israelites as God's covenant people. The name "uncircumcised" was a term of reproach, similar to the names that people use today for despised nationalities. We can feel something of its sting when we hear David say concerning the Gentile Goliath, "Who is this uncircumcised Philistine that he should defy the armies of the living God?" (I Sam. 17:26, RSV).

The Jews, by contrast, spoke of themselves as the "Circumcision." This was a name of which they were proud. It identified them as God's chosen earthly people, set apart from all the other nations of the earth.

Paul seems to take exception to some of their boasting by saying that their circumcision was only "in the flesh made by hands." It was merely physical. / Though they had the outward sign of God's covenant people, they did not have the inward reality of true faith in the Lord. "For he is not a Jew, which is one outwardly; neither is that circumcision, which is outward in the flesh: but he is a Jew, which is one inwardly; and circumcision is that of the heart, in the spirit, and not in the letter; whose praise is not of men, but of God" (Rom. 2:28-29).

But whether or not the Jews were circumcised in heart, the point in this verse is that in their own eyes they were *the* people and the Gentiles were despised. This enmity between Jews and Gentiles was the greatest racial and religious difference that the world has ever known. The Jew enjoyed a position of great privilege before God (Rom. 9:4-5). The Gentile was a foreigner. If he wanted to worship the true God in the appointed way, he actually had to become a Jewish convert (cf. Rahab and Ruth). The Jewish temple in Jerusalem was the only place on earth where God had placed His name and where men could approach Him. Gentiles were forbidden to enter the inner temple area on pain of death.

In His interview with a Gentile woman from the region of Tyre and Sidon, the Lord Jesus tested her faith by picturing the Jews as children in the house and the Gentiles as stray dogs. She acknowledged that she was only a puppy, but asked for some crumbs the children might drop. Needless to say, her faith was rewarded (Mark 7:24-30).

Here in Ephesians 2:11 the apostle is reminding his readers that they were formerly Gentiles and therefore despised.

2:12   The Gentiles were also without Christ. This means that they were without the Messiah. It was to the nation of Israel that He was promised. Although it was predicted that blessing would flow to the nations through the ministry of the Messiah (Isa. 11:10; 60:3), yet He was to be born a Jew and to minister primarily "to the lost sheep of the house of Israel" (Matt. 15:24).

In addition to being without the Messiah, the Gentiles were "aliens from the commonwealth of Israel." An alien is one who does not "belong." He is a stranger and a foreigner, without the rights and privileges of citizenship. As far as the community of Israel was concerned, the Gentiles were on the outside, looking in.

And they were "strangers from the covenants of promise." God had made convenants with the nation of Israel through such men as Abraham, Isaac, Jacob, Moses, David and Solomon. These covenants promised blessings to the Jews. For all practical purposes, the Gentiles were outside the pale.

They were without hope, both nationally and individually. Nationally, they had no assurance that their land, their government or their people would survive. And individually their outlook was bleak; they had no hope beyond the grave. Someone has said that their future was a night without a star.

Finally, they were "without God in the world." This does not mean that they were atheists. They had their own gods of wood and stone, and worshiped them. But they did not know the one and only true God. They were God-less in a godless, hostile world.

2:13 The words "But now" signal another abrupt transition (cf. 2:4). The Ephesian Gentiles had been rescued from that place of distance and alienation, and had been elevated to a position of nearness to God.

This was brought about at the time of their conversion. When they trusted the Savior, God placed them "in Christ" and accepted them in the beloved One. From then on, they were as near to God as Christ is, because they were *in Christ*.

The cost of effecting this marvelous change was the blood of Christ. Before these Gentile sinners could enjoy the privilege of nearness to God, they had to be cleansed from their sins. Only the blood of Christ shed at Calvary could do this. When they received the Lord Jesus by a definite act of faith, all the cleansing value of His precious blood was credited to their account.

The Lord Jesus not only brought them near; He also created a new society in which the ancient enmity between Jew and Gentile was forever abolished. Up to New Testament times, all the world was divided into two classes—Jew and Gentile. Our Savior has introduced a third—the church of God (I Cor. 10:32). In the verses that follow we see how believing Jews and believing Gentiles are now made one in Christ, and are introduced into this new society where there is neither Jew nor Gentile.

2:14 "For he is our peace." Notice that it does not say, "He made peace." That, of course, is true too, as we will see in the next verse. Here the fact is that He *is* our peace.

But how? How can a person be peace?

This is how: When a Jew believes on the Lord Jesus, he loses his national identity; from then on, he is "in Christ." Likewise, when a Gentile receives the Savior, he is no longer a Gentile; henceforth, he is "in Christ." In other words, believing Jew and believing Gentile, once divided by enmity, are now one in Christ. Their union with Christ necessarily

unites them with one another. Therefore a man is the peace,
just as Micah predicted (Micah 5:5).

The scope of His work as our peace is detailed in verses
14-18.

First is the work of union which we have just described.
He has made both one—that is, both believing Jews and
believing Gentiles. They are no longer Jews or Gentiles but
Christians. Strictly speaking, it is not accurate even to speak
of them as Jewish Christians or Gentile Christians. All fleshly
distinctions, such as nationality, were nailed to the cross.

The second phase of Christ's work might be called demoli-
tion; "he . . . hath broken down the middle wall of partition."
Not a literal wall, of course, but the invisible barrier set up
by the Mosaic law of commandments contained in ordinances
which partitioned the people of Israel from the nations. This
has often been illustrated by the wall which restricted non-
Jews to the Court of the Gentiles in the temple area. On the
wall were No Trespassing signs which read: "Let no one of
any other nation come within the fence and barrier around
the Holy Place. Whosoever will be taken doing so will himself be responsible for the fact that his death will ensue."

2:15 A third aspect of Christ's work was abolition of the
enmity that raged between Jew and Gentile and also between
man and God. Paul identifies the law as the innocent cause
of the enmity: "even the law of commandments contained in
ordinances." The law of Moses was a single legislative code;
yet it was made up of separate, formal commandments; these
in turn consisted of dogmas or decrees covering many if not
most areas of life. The law itself was holy, just and good
(Rom. 7:12), but man's sinful nature used the law as an occasion for hatred. Because the law actually did set up Israel
as God's chosen earthly people, the Jews became arrogant
and treated the Gentiles with contempt. The Gentiles struck
back with deep hostility, which we have come to know all too
well as anti-Semitism.

But how did Christ remove the law as the cause of enmity?
First, He died to pay the penalty of the law that had been

broken. He thus completely satisfied the righteous claim of God. Now the law has nothing more to say to those who are "in Christ"; the penalty has been paid for them in full. Believers are not under law but under grace. However, this does not mean that they can live as they please; it means that they are now enlawed to Christ, and should live as He pleases.

As a result of abolishing the hostility stirred up by the law, the Lord has been able to usher in a new creation. He has made in Himself of the two, that is, of believing Jew and Gentile, one new man—the church. Through union with Him, the former combatants are united with one another in this new fellowship.

The church is new in the sense that it is a new kind of organism that never existed before. It is important to see this. The New Testament church is not a continuation of the Israel of the Old Testament. It is something entirely distinct from anything that has preceded it or that will ever follow it. This should be apparent from the following:

1. It is new that a Gentile should have equal rights and privileges with a Jew.
2. It is new that both Jews and Gentiles should lose their national identities by becoming Christians.
3. It is new that Jews and Gentiles should be fellow members of the body of Christ.
4. It is new that a Jew should have the hope of reigning with Christ instead of being a subject in His kingdom.
5. It is new that a Jew should no longer be under the law.

The church is clearly a new creation, with a distinct calling and a distinct destiny, occupying a unique place in the purposes of God.

But the scope of Christ's work does not stop there. He has also made peace between Jew and Gentile. He did this by removing the cause of hostility, by imparting a new nature and by creating a new union.

The cross is God's answer to racial discrimination, segregation, anti-Semitism, bigotry and every form of strife between men.

2:16   In addition to reconciling Jew and Gentile to one another, Christ has reconciled them both to God. Though Israel and the nations were normally bitterly opposed to each other, there was one sense in which they were united—in their hostility to God. The cause of this hostility was sin. By His death on the cross, the Lord Jesus removed the enmity by removing the cause. Those who receive Him are reckoned righteous, forgiven, redeemed, pardoned and delivered from the power of sin. The enmity is gone; now they have peace with God.

The Lord Jesus unites believing Jew and Gentile in one body, the church, and presents this body to God with all trace of antagonism gone.

God never needed to be reconciled to us; He never hated us. But we needed to be reconciled to Him. The work of our Lord on the cross provided a righteous basis upon which we could be brought into His presence as friends, not as foes.

2:17   In verse 14 we learned that Christ *is* our peace. In verse 15 we read that He *made* peace. Now we find that He came and *preached* peace.

When and how did He come? First, He came personally in resurrection. Second, He came representatively by the Holy Spirit.

He preached peace in resurrection; in fact, peace was one of the first words He spoke after rising from the dead (Luke 24:36; John 20:19, 21, 26). Then He sent forth the apostles in the power of the Holy Spirit and preached peace through them (Acts 10:36).

The good news of peace was presented to "you which were far off" (Gentiles) and "to them that were nigh" (Jews), a gracious fulfillment of God's promise in Isaiah 57:19.

2:18   The practical proof that a state of peace now exists between members of the one body and God is that they have access at any time into the presence of God. This is in sharp contrast to the Old Testament economy where only the high priest could go into the Holy of Holies, the place of God's presence. And He could enter there on only one day of the year. "Now the most distant Gentile who is in Christ really and continually enjoys that august spiritual privilege which the one man of the one tribe of the one nation on the one day of the year, only typically and periodically possessed" (Eadie). Through prayer, he can enter the throne room of heaven, kneel down before the Sovereign of the universe, and address Him as "my Father."

The normal order to be followed in prayer is given here. First of all, it is "through Him," that is, through the Lord Jesus. He is the one Mediator between God and man. His death, burial and resurrection removed every legal obstacle to our admission to God's presence. Now as Mediator, He lives on high to maintain us in a condition of fellowship with the Father. We approach God in His name; we have no worthiness of our own so we plead His worthiness.

The participants in prayer are "we both"—believing Jews and Gentiles.

The privilege is that we "have our access" (RV).

Our Helper in prayer is the Holy Spirit—"by one Spirit." "The Spirit also helpeth our infirmity: for we know not how to pray as we ought; but the Spirit himself maketh intercession for us with groanings which cannot be uttered" (Rom. 8:26, RV).

The One we approach is the Father. No Old Testament saint ever knew God as Father. Before the resurrection of Christ, men stood before God as creatures before the Creator. It was only after He rose that He said, "Go to my brethren, and say unto them, I ascend unto my Father, and your Father; and to my God, and your God" (John 20:17). As a result of His redemptive work, believers were then able for the first time to address God as Father.

Thus we see in verse 18 that all three Persons of the Trinity are directly involved in the prayers of the humblest believer;

he prays to God the Father, approaching Him through the
Lord Jesus Christ, in the power of the Holy Spirit.

2:19 In the last four verses of this chapter, the Apostle
Paul lists some of the overwhelming new privileges of believing Gentiles.

They are no longer strangers and foreigners. Never again
will they be aliens, dogs, uncircumcision, outsiders.

Now they are fellow citizens with all the saints of the New
Testament period. Believers of Jewish ancestry have no ad-
vantage over them. All Christians are first-class citizens of
heaven (Phil. 3:20-21, ASV).

They are also members of the household of God. Not only
have they been supernaturalized into the divine kingdom;
they have been adopted into the divine family.

2:20 Finally, they have been made members of the
church, or as Paul pictures it here, they have become stones
in the construction of a holy temple. With great detail the
apostle describes this temple—its foundation, its chief cornerstone, its cohesive agent, its unity and symmetry, its growth,
and its other unique features.

This temple is built upon the foundation of the apostles
and prophets. This refers to the apostles and prophets of the
New Testament era; it could not possibly refer to Old Testament prophets because they knew nothing about the church.
It does not mean that the apostles and prophets were the
foundation of the church. Christ is the foundation (Rom.
15:20; I Cor. 3:11). But they laid the foundation in what
they taught about the person and work of the Lord Jesus.
The church is founded on Christ as He was revealed by the
confession and teaching of the apostles and prophets. When
Peter confessed Him as the Christ, the Son of the living God,
Jesus announced that His church would be built upon that
rock, namely, on the solid truth that He is the anointed of
God and God's unique Son (Matt. 16:18). In Revelation
21:14, the apostles are associated with the twelve foundations
of the holy Jerusalem. They are not the foundation but are

linked with it because they first taught the great truth concerning Christ and the church.

The foundation of a building needs to be laid only once. The apostles and prophets did this work once for all. The foundation they laid is preserved for us in the writings of the New Testament, though they themselves are with us no longer.

Christ Jesus is not only the foundation of the temple; He is its chief cornerstone as well. Those who contend that He cannot be both fail to realize that no one picture or type can adequately portray Him in His manifold glories or in His varied ministries.

There are at least three possible explanations of the chief cornerstone, all of which point to the Lord Jesus Christ as the unique, preeminent and indispensable Head of the church.

1. We generally think of the cornerstone as one that lies at a lower front corner of a building. Since the rest of the structure seems to be supported by it, it has come to signify something of fundamental importance. In that sense it is a true type of the Lord. Also since it joins two walls together, there may be a suggestion of the union of believing Jews and Gentiles in the church through Him.

2. Some Bible students believe that the chief cornerstone is the keystone of an arch. This stone occupies the highest place in the arch and provides support for the other stones. So Christ is the preeminent One in the church. He is also the indispensable One; remove Him and the rest will collapse.

3. A third possible explanation of the chief cornerstone is that it is the capstone of a pyramid. This stone occupies the highest place in the structure. It is the only stone of that size and shape. And its angles and lines determine the shape of the whole pyramid. So Christ is the Head of the church. He is unique as to His person and ministry. And He is the One who gives the church its unique character.

2:21 "In whom all the building fitted together increases to a holy temple in the Lord" (JND).

The words "in whom" refer to Christ; He is the source of the church's life and growth. "In Him we are added to it; in Him we grow in it; in Him the whole temple grows toward the final consummation when the topstone shall be brought out with shouts of 'Grace, grace unto it' " (Pulpit Commentary).

The unity and symmetry of the temple are indicated by the expression, "All the building fitted together." It is a unity made up of many individual members. Each member has a specific place in the building for which he is exactly suited. Stones excavated from the valley of death by the grace of God are found to fit together perfectly.

The unique feature of this building is that it grows. However, this feature is not the same as the growth of a building through the addition of bricks and cement. Think of it rather as the growth of a living organism, such as the human body. After all, the church is not an inanimate building. Neither is it an organization. It is a living entity with Christ as its Head and all believers forming the body. It was born on the day of Pentecost, has been growing ever since, and will continue to grow until the rapture.

This growing building of living materials is described as a holy temple in the Lord. The word Paul used for temple referred not to the outer courts but to the inner shrine, not the suburbs but the sanctuary. He was thinking of the main building of the temple complex which housed the Most Holy Place. There God dwelt and there He manifested Himself in a bright, shining cloud of glory.

There are several lessons for us here:

1. God indwells the church. Saved Jews and Gentiles form a living sanctuary in which He dwells and where He manifests His glory.
2. This temple is holy. It is set apart from the world and dedicated to Him for sacred purposes.
3. As a holy temple, the church is a center from which

praise, worship and adoration ascend to God through the Lord Jesus Christ.

Paul further describes it as a holy temple *in the Lord.* In other words, the Lord Jesus is its source of holiness. Its members are holy positionally through union with Him and they should be holy practically out of love to Him.

2:22 In this wonderful temple, believing Gentiles have an equal place with believing Jews. It should thrill us to read this, as it must have thrilled the Ephesians and others when they heard it for the first time.

The tremendous dignity of the believers' position is that they form "a habitation of God in the Spirit." This is the purpose of the temple—to provide a place where God can dwell in fellowship with His people. The church is that place.

Compare this with the position of the Gentiles in the Old Testament. At that time they could not get near the habitation of God. Now they themselves *form* the habitation of God.

And notice the ministry of each of the Persons of the Godhead in connection with the church (v. 22).

1. "In whom," that is, in Christ. It is through union with Him that we are built into the temple.
2. "A habitation of God." This temple is the dwelling place of God the Father on earth.
3. "In the Spirit" (RSV). It is in the Person of the Holy Spirit that God indwells the church (I Cor. 3:16).

And so the chapter that began with a description of Gentiles who were dead, depraved, diabolical and disobedient, closes with those same Gentiles cleansed from all guilt and defilement, and forming a habitation of God through the Spirit.

3

VI. A Parenthesis on the Mystery (3:1-13)

    A. The Apostle of the Mystery (v. 1): *For this cause I Paul, the prisoner of Christ Jesus on behalf of you Gentiles* (RV)

    B. The Nature of His Ministry (v. 2)
        1. A stewardship: *assuming that you have heard of the stewardship* (RSV)
        2. Its source and substance: *[the stewardship] of God's grace* (RSV)
        3. Its steward: *that was given to me [Paul]* (RSV)
        4. Its sphere: *for you [Gentiles]* (RSV)

    C. The Manner in Which He Received the Mystery (v. 3a): *How that by revelation he made known unto me the mystery*

    D. The Proof of His Knowledge of the Mystery (vv. 3b-4): *as I wrote afore in few words, Whereby, when ye read, ye may understand my knowledge in the mystery of Christ*

    E. The Definition of the Mystery (vv. 5-6)
        1. A truth hitherto unknown (v. 5): *Which in other ages was not made known unto the sons of men*
        2. A truth now disclosed by the Spirit (v. 5): *as it is now revealed unto his holy apostles and prophets by the Spirit*
        3. The truth that believing Gentiles now have full and equal privileges (v. 6)
            a. Fellow heirs: *that the Gentiles are fellow-heirs* (RV)
            b. Fellow members: *and fellow-members of the body* (RV)
            c. Fellow partakers: *and fellow-partakers of the promise in Christ Jesus through the gospel* (RV)

F. The Gospel and Its Ministry (vv. 7-9): *Whereof I was made a minister*

1. An unearned gift (v. 7): *according to the GIFT of the grace of God given unto me*
2. An effective power (v. 7): *by the effectual working of his power*
3. An unworthy recipient (v. 8): *Unto me, who am less than the least of all saints, is this grace given*
4. A twofold privilege and responsibility (vv. 8-9)
   a. The gospel: *that I should preach among the Gentiles the unsearchable riches of Christ*
   b. The church: *and to enlighten all with the knowledge of what is the administration of the mystery hidden throughout the ages in God, who has created all things* (JND)

G. A Present Purpose of the Mystery: (vv. 10-11)

1. The spectators (v. 10): *To the intent that now unto the principalities and powers*
2. Their locale (v. 10): *in heavenly places*
3. The object on display (v. 10): *might be known by the church*
4. The lesson (v. 10): *the manifold wisdom of God*
5. The origin of the plan (v. 11): *According to the eternal purpose*
6. The One by whom He brought it to pass (v. 11): *which he has realized in Christ Jesus our Lord* (RSV)

H. A Present Benefit of Christ's Work for Us (v. 12)

1. The source: *In whom [Christ]*
2. The recipients: *we [all believers]*
3. The benefit: *have boldness and access with confidence*
4. The means: *through our faith in him* (RV)

I. A request from Paul, the prisoner (v. 13)

1. Negative: *Wherefore I desire that ye faint not at my tribulations for you*
2. Positive: *which is your glory*

3:1 In this verse, Paul begins a statement that is interrupted in verse 2 and not resumed until verse 14. The intervening verses form a parenthesis, the theme of which is the mystery—Christ and the church.

What makes this of special interest is that this present Church Age is itself a parenthesis in God's dealings. This can be explained as follows: During most of the period of history recorded in the Old Testament, God was dealing primarily with the Jewish people. In fact, from Genesis 12 through Malachi 4 the narrative centers almost exclusively on Abraham and his descendants. When the Lord Jesus came to earth, He was rejected by Israel. As a result, God set aside that nation temporarily as His chosen, earthly people. We are now living in the Church Age when Jews and Gentiles are on the same level before God.

After the church has been completed and is taken home to heaven, God will resume His program with Israel nationally. The hands on the prophetic clock will begin to move once more.

So the present age is sort of a parenthesis between God's past and future dealings with Israel. It is a new administration in the divine program—unique and separate from anything before or after it.

Now in verses 2-13, Paul is going to give us a fairly detailed explanation of this parenthesis. Is it an undesigned coincidence that in doing so he uses a literary parenthesis to explain a dispensational parenthesis?

The apostle opens the section, "For this cause, I Paul, the prisoner of Christ Jesus in behalf of you Gentiles. . . ." The phrase "For this cause. . . ." looks back to what he had just been saying about the place of privilege into which believing Gentiles are brought as a result of their union with Christ.

It is generally believed that this letter was written during Paul's first Roman imprisonment. But he does not speak of himself as a prisoner of Rome. That might have indicated a sense of defeat, a feeling of self-pity or a craving for sympathy. Paul calls himself a prisoner of Christ Jesus; this speaks of acceptance and dignity and triumph. "There is no smell of a prison in Ephesians, for Paul is not bound in spirit. He is there as the prisoner of Rome, but this he will not admit, and claims to be the prisoner of Jesus Christ. What is the secret of such victorious other-worldliness? Paul's spirit is with Christ in the heavenlies, though his body languishes in prison" (Paxson).

His imprisonment was definitely on behalf of the Gentiles. Throughout his ministry he ran into bitter opposition for teaching that believing Gentiles now enjoyed equal rights and privileges with believing Jews in the Christian church. What finally triggered his arrest and his trial before Caesar was a false charge that he had taken Trophimus, an Ephesian, into the temple area that was out of bounds for Gentiles (Acts 21:29). But behind the charge was the already fierce hostility of the religious leaders.

3:2 Now Paul breaks the train of his thought and launches into a discourse on the mystery, in what we have already referred to as a literary parenthesis dealing with a dispensational parenthesis.

The "if" in verse 2 ("if ye have heard. . . .") might create the impression that the apostle's readers did not know of his special mission to the Gentiles. In fact, this verse is sometimes used to prove that Paul did not know the persons to whom he wrote and that therefore the letter could not have been written to the beloved Ephesians. But "if" often carries the meaning of "since." Thus Phillips paraphrases it "For you must have heard. . . ." They had surely known that this special ministry had been committed to him.

He describes that ministry as a "stewardship of God's grace" (RSV). A steward, of course, is one who is appointed to administer the affairs of someone else. Paul was God's steward, charged with setting forth the great truth regarding the New Testament assembly. It was a stewardship of God's grace in at least three senses:

1. As to the one chosen. It was undeserved favor to Paul that selected him for such a high privilege.

2. As to the contents of the message. It was the message of God's free and unmerited kindness.
3. As to its recipients. The Gentiles were quite unworthy people to be so favored.

Yet this stewardship of grace was given to Paul in order that he in turn might impart it to the Gentiles.

3:3 He had not learned the mystery from any other man, nor had he discovered it through his own intelligence. It was made known to him by direct revelation from God. We are not told where this happened, or how; all we know is that in some miraculous way God showed Paul His plan for a church composed of converted Jews and converted Gentiles.

We have already mentioned that a mystery is a sacred secret hitherto unknown, humanly unknowable, and now divinely revealed.

The apostle had alluded to the mystery briefly in 1:9-14, 22-23; 2:11-22.

3:4 What he had already written on the subject was sufficient to demonstrate to his readers that he had a God-given insight into the mystery of the Christ (JND).

The Pulpit Commentary paraphrases this passage as follows: "With reference to what I wrote afore, to make that more intelligible, I write on the subject more fully now so that you shall see that your instructor is thoroughly informed in this matter of the mystery. . . ."

Darby's translation "the mystery of *the* Christ" suggests that it is the mystical Christ that is in view here, that is, the Head *and* the body. (For another instance of the name *Christ* including both the Lord Jesus and His people, see I Cor. 12:12, JND.)

3:5 Verses 5 and 6 give us the most complete definition of the mystery which we have. Paul explains what a mystery is, then he explains what the mystery of the Christ is.

First we learn that it is a truth which in other ages was not made known to the sons of men. This means that it is futile to look for it in the Old Testament. There may be types and pictures of it there but the truth itself was unknown at that time.

Second, we learn that it is a truth which has now been disclosed to God's holy apostles and prophets by the Holy Spirit. God was the Revealer; the apostles and prophets were the ones who were set apart to receive the revelation; the Holy Spirit was the channel through whom the revelation came to them.

Unless we see that the apostles and prophets were those of the New Testament, not the Old Testament period, this verse is contradictory. The first part says that this truth was not revealed in other ages; therefore it was unknown to the Old Testament prophets. How then could it be made known in Paul's day to men who had been dead for centuries? The obvious meaning is that the great truth of Christ and the church was made known to men of the Church Age like Paul who were specially commissioned by the risen Lord to serve as His spokesmen or mouthpieces.

(Notice that Paul does not claim to be the only one to whom this sacred secret was disclosed; he was one among many, though he was the foremost in transmitting the truth to Gentiles of his day, and to succeeding generations through his epistles.)

Before leaving verse 5, we must mention that many Christians take quite a different view from that given above. They say that the church actually did exist in the Old Testament; that Israel was then the church; but that the truth of the church has now been more fully revealed. They say, "The mystery was not known in other ages *as* it is now revealed. It was known *but not to the same extent as now.* We have a *fuller revelation,* but we are still the Israel of God, that is, a continuation of God's people."

To clinch their argument, they point to Acts 7:38 where the nation of Israel is called "the church in the wilderness."

It is true that God's chosen people are spoken of as the church in the wilderness, but this does not mean that they have any connection with the Christian church. After all, the word *church* (Greek: *ecclesia*) is a general term which means any assembly, congregation or called-out group. It is not only applied to Israel in Acts 7:38; the same word, translated *assembly*, is used in Acts 19:32, 41, of a heathen mob. We have to determine from the context *which* church or assembly is meant.

But what about the argument that verse 5 means that the church existed in the Old Testament though it was not as fully revealed then as now? This is answered in Colossians 1:26, which states flatly that the mystery was hidden from ages and from generations but now is made manifest to His saints. It is not a question of the degree of revelation but of the fact itself.

3:6 Now we come to the central truth of the mystery, namely, that in the church of the Lord Jesus Christ believing Gentiles are fellow heirs, fellow members, and fellow partakers of His promise in Christ by the gospel. In other words, converted Gentiles now enjoy equal title and privileges with converted Jews.

First of all, they are fellow heirs. As far as the inheritance is concerned, they share equally with saved Jews. They are heirs of God, joint heirs with Jesus Christ and fellow heirs with all the redeemed.

Then they are fellow members of the body. They are at no distance or disadvantage now, but share a position of equality with saved Jews in the church.

Finally, they are fellow partakers of the promise in Christ Jesus through the gospel. The promise here may mean the Holy Spirit (Acts 15:8; Gal. 3:14), or it may take in all that is promised in the gospel to those who are in Christ Jesus. Gentiles are copartners with Jews in all of this.

None of this was true in the Old Testament dispensation, nor will it be true in the coming kingdom of Christ.

In the Old Testament, Israel held a distinct place of privilege before God. A Jew would have laughed at any suggestion that a Gentile held an equal share with him in the promises of God. It simply was not true. The prophets of Israel did predict the call of the Gentiles (Isa. 49:6; 56:6-7), but they nowhere hinted that Gentiles would be fellow members of a body in which Jews did not have any priority.

In the coming kingdom of our Lord, Israel will be the head of the nations (Isa. 60:12); Gentiles will be blessed but it will be through Israel (Isa. 60:3; 61:6; Zech. 8:23).

The calling of Israel was primarily, though not exclusively, to temporal blessings in earthly places (Deut. 28; Amos 9:13-15). The calling of the church is to spiritual blessings in heavenly places (Eph. 1:3). Israel was called to be God's chosen earthly people. The church is called to be the heavenly bride of Christ (Rev. 21:9-11, 22-23). Israel will be blessed under the rule of Christ in the millennium (Hosea 3:5); the church will reign with Him over the entire universe, sharing His glory (Eph. 1:22-23).

Therefore it should be clear that the church is not the same as Israel and it is not the same as the kingdom. It is a new society, a unique fellowship, and the most privileged body of believers we read about in the Bible. The church came into being after Christ ascended and the Holy Spirit was given (Acts 2). It was formed by the baptism of the Holy Spirit (I Cor. 12:13). And it will be completed at the rapture when all who belong to Christ will be taken home to heaven (I Thess. 4:13-18; I Cor. 15:23, 51-52).

3:7 Having emphasized the equal partnership of Gentiles and Jews in the church, Paul now moves on to discuss his own ministry in connection with it (vv. 7-9).

First of all, he was made a minister of the gospel. "The word 'minister' is misleading, since it is the technical word used today to designate the pastor of a church" (Wuest). It never means that in the New Testament. The basic meaning of the word is servant; Paul simply meant that he served the Lord in connection with the mystery.

The ministry was in the nature of an undeserved gift: "according to the gift of the grace of God given unto me." And it was not only a display of grace; it also demonstrated God's power in effectually reaching the proud, self-righteous Pharisee, saving his soul, commissioning him as an apostle, empowering him to receive revelations, and strengthening him for the work. So Paul says that the gift was given to him "by the effectual working of his power."

3:8   The apostle speaks of himself as "less than the least of all saints." This might seem like mock humility to some. Actually it is the true self-estimate of one who is filled by the Holy Spirit. Anyone who sees Christ in His glory realizes his own sinfulness and uselessness. In Paul's case there was the added memory that he had persecuted the Lord Jesus (Acts 9:4) by persecuting the church of God (Gal. 1:13; Phil. 3:6).

In spite of this, the Lord had commissioned him in a special way to take the gospel to the Gentiles (Acts 9:15; 13:47; 22:21; Gal. 2:2, 8). Paul was the apostle to the Gentiles as Peter was to the Jews.

His ministry was twofold; it concerned the gospel, and it concerned the church. First, he told men how to be saved, then he led them on into the truth of the New Testament church. For him evangelism was not an end in itself but a step toward the establishment and strengthening of indigenous New Testament churches.

The first function of his ministry was to preach among the Gentiles the unsearchable riches of Christ. "Two attractive words: *riches* and *unsearchable*, conveying the idea of the things that are most precious being infinitely abundant. Usually precious things are rare; their very rarity increases their price; but here that which is most precious is also boundless—riches of compassion and love, of merit, of sanctifying, comforting and transforming power, all without limit and capable of satisfying every want, craving and yearning of the heart, now and evermore" (Pulpit Commentary).

When a person trusts the Lord Jesus, he immediately becomes a spiritual billionaire; in Christ he possesses inexhaustible treasures.

3:9 The second part of Paul's ministry was to make all men see what is "the administration of the mystery" (JND), in other words, to enlighten them as to how the mystery is being worked out in practice. God's plan for this present age is to call out of the Gentiles a people for His name (Acts 15:14), a bride for His Son. All that is involved in this plan is the administration of the mystery.

"All men" here means all believers. Unsaved people could not be expected to understand the deep truths of the mystery (I Cor. 2:14). Paul therefore is referring to all men in the sense of saved men of all kinds—Jews and Gentiles, slave and free.

This mystery has been hidden in God from all ages. The plan itself was in the mind of God eternally, but here the thought is that He kept it a secret throughout the ages of human history. Once again we notice the care which the Holy Spirit takes to impress us with the fact that the assembly, or church universal, is something new, unique, unprecedented. It was not known before to anyone but God.

The secret was hidden "in God who created all things." He created the material universe, He created the ages, and He created the church—but in His wisdom He decided to withhold any knowledge of this new creation until the first advent of Christ.

3:10 One of God's present purposes in connection with the mystery is to reveal His manifold wisdom to the angelic hosts of heaven. The apostle again uses the metaphor of a school. God is the Teacher. The universe is the classroom. Angelic dignitaries are the students. The lesson is on "The multi-faceted wisdom of God." The church is the object lesson.

From heaven, the angels are compelled to admire His unsearchable judgments and marvel at His ways past finding out. They see how God has triumphed over sin to His own glory. They see how He has sent heaven's best for earth's worst. They see how He has redeemed His enemies at enormous cost, conquered them by love, and prepared them as a bride for His Son. They see how He has blessed them with all spiritual blessings in the heavenlies. And they see that through the work of the Lord Jesus on the cross, more glory has come to God and more blessing has come to believing Jews and Gentiles than if sin had never been allowed to enter. God has been vindicated; Christ has been exalted; Satan has been defeated; and the church has been enthroned in Christ to share His glory.

3:11   The mystery itself, its concealment, its eventual disclosure, and the manner in which it exhibits the wisdom of God are all "according to the eternal purpose which He purposed in Christ Jesus our Lord." Before the world was made, God knew that Satan would fall and that man would follow Him in sin. And He had already prepared a counter-strategy, a master plan. This plan has been worked out in the incarnation, death, resurrection, ascension and glorification of Christ. The whole program centered in Christ and has been realized through Him. Now God can save ungodly Jews and Gentiles, make them members of the body of Christ, conform them to the image of His Son, and honor them in a unique way as the bride of the Lamb throughout eternity.

3:12   As a result of Christ's work and of our union with Him, we now have the unspeakable privilege of entering into God's presence at any time, in full confidence of being heard, and without any fear of being scolded (James 1:5).

Our access is our liberty to speak to God in prayer. Our boldness is the respectful attitude and the absence of fear we have as children addressing their Father. Our confidence is the assurance of a welcome, a hearing and a wise and loving answer. And it is all "through our faith in Him" (RV), that is, our faith in **the Lord Jesus Christ**.

3:13 In view of the dignity of his ministry and the wonderful results that flowed from it, Paul encouraged the saints not to be disheartened when they thought of his sufferings. He was glad to endure tribulations in carrying out his mission to the Gentiles. Rather than being discouraged by his troubles, he says in effect, they should be proud that he was counted worthy to suffer for the Lord Jesus. They should rejoice to think of the benefit of his tribulations to them and to other Gentiles. They should see his current imprisonment as glory, not disgrace.

VII. Paul's Prayer for the Saints (3:14-19)

    A. The Posture of Prayer (v. 14): *For this cause I bow my knees*

    B. The Person Addressed (v. 14): *unto the Father* (RV)

    C. The Particular Role of God in View (v. 15): *of whom the whole family in heaven and earth is named*

    D. The Plenitude of the Things Requested (v. 16): *That he would grant you, according to the riches of his glory*

    E. The Specific Requests (vv. 16-19)
        1. For spiritual strength (v. 16): *to be strengthened with might by his Spirit in the inner man*
        2. For the enjoyment of Christ's indwelling (v. 17): *That Christ may dwell in your hearts by faith*
        3. For establishment in love (v. 17): *That ye, being rooted and grounded in love*
        4. For understanding of the dimensions of the mystery (v. 18): *May be able to apprehend with all saints what is the breadth, and length, and depth, and height* (FWG)
        5. For appreciation of the knowledge-surpassing love of Christ (v. 19): *And to know the love of Christ, which passeth knowledge*
        6. For lives filled unto all the fullness of God (v. 19): *that ye may be filled unto all the fulness of God* (RV)

3:14 Now the apostle picks up the thought which he had begun in verse 1 and which he had interrupted with a parenthetical section on the mystery. Therefore, the words *"For this cause. . . ."* refer back to chapter 2 with its description of what the Gentiles had been by nature and what they had become through union with Christ. Their astonishing rise from poverty and death to riches and glory drives Paul to pray that they will always live in the practical enjoyment of their exalted position.

His posture in prayer is indicated: "I bow my knees." This does not mean that kneeling must always be the posture of the body, though it should always be the posture of the soul. We may pray as we walk, sit or recline, but our spirits should be bowed in humility and reverence.

The prayer is addressed to the Father. In a general sense, God is the Father of all mankind, meaning that He is their Creator (Acts 17:28-29). In a more restricted sense, He is the Father of all believers, meaning that He has begotten them into His spiritual family (Gal. 4:6). In a unique sense He is the Father of the Lord Jesus, meaning that They are equal (John 5:18).

3:15 The particular role of the Father which Paul has in view is as the One "from whom every family in heaven and on earth is named" (RSV). This may mean that:

1. All the redeemed in heaven and on earth look to Him as Head of the family.
2. All created beings, angelic and human, owe their existence to Him not only as individuals but as families as well. Families in heaven include the various grades of angelic creatures. Families on earth are the different races springing from Noah and now divided into various nations.
3. All fatherhood in the universe derives its name from Him. The Fatherhood of God is the original and the ideal; it is the prototype of every other paternal relationship. Phillips translates the verse, "from whom all fatherhood, earthly or heavenly, derives its name."

3:16 We cannot help but be struck by the vastness of Paul's request: "That he would grant you, *according to the riches of his glory.*" He is going to ask that the saints might be spiritually strengthened. But to what extent? "Not according to the narrowness of our hearts but in abundance consonant to the riches of His glory" (Jamieson, Fausset and Brown).

It has often been pointed out that there is a difference between the expressions "out of the riches" and "according to the riches." A wealthy person might give a trifling amount; it would be out of his riches, but not in proportion to them. Paul asks that God will give strength *according to* the riches of His perfections. Since the Lord is infinitely rich in glory, let the saints get ready for a deluge!

Why should we ask so little of so great a King? When someone asked a tremendous favor of Napoleon it was immediately granted because, said Napoleon, "He honored me by the magnitude of his request."

> Thou art coming to a King;
> Large petitions with thee bring:
> For His grace and power are such,
> None can ever ask too much.

Now we come to the apostle's specific prayer requests. Instead of a series of disconnected petitions, we should think of them as a progression in which each petition lays the groundwork for the next. Picture them as a pyramid: the first request is the bottom layer of stones. As the prayer advances, Paul builds toward a glorious climax.

The first request is "that ye may be strengthened with power through the Spirit in the inward man" (RV). The blessing sought is spiritual might. Not the power to perform spectacular miracles, but the spiritual vigor needed to be mature, stable, intelligent Christians.

The One who imparts this power is the Holy Spirit. Of course, He can give us strength only as we feed on the Word of God, as we breathe the pure air of prayer, and as we get exercise in daily service for the Lord.

This power is experienced in the inward man, that is, the spiritual part of our nature. It is the inward man that delights in the law of God (Rom. 7:22). It is the inward man that is renewed day by day, even though the outward man is perishing (II Cor. 4:16). Though it is of God, our inward man needs strength, growth and development.

3:17 The second step is "that Christ may dwell in your hearts by faith." This is the result of the Spirit's invigoration; we are strengthened in order that Christ may dwell in our hearts.

Actually, the Lord Jesus takes up His personal residence in a believer at the time of conversion (John 14:23; Rev. 3:20). But that is not the subject of this prayer. Here it is not a question of His being in the believer, but rather of His feeling at home there. He is a permanent Resident in every saved person, but this is a request that He might have full access to every room and closet; that He might not be grieved by sinful words, thoughts, motives and deeds; that He might enjoy unbroken fellowship with the believer.

The Christian heart thus becomes the home of Christ, the place where He loves to be—like the home of Mary, Martha and Lazarus in Bethany. The heart, of course, means the center of the spiritual life; it controls every aspect of behavior. In effect, the apostle prays that the lordship of Christ might extend to the books we read, the work we do, the food we eat, the money we spend, the words we speak—in short, the minutest details of our lives.

The more we are strengthened by the Holy Spirit, the more we will be like the Lord Jesus Himself. And the more we are like Him, the more He will "settle down and feel completely at home in our hearts" (KSW).

We enter into the enjoyment of His indwelling by faith. This involves constant dependence on Him, constant surrender to Him, and constant recognition of His "at homeness." It is by faith that we practice His presence, as Brother Lawrence quaintly put it.

Up to this point, Paul's prayer has involved each member

of the Trinity. The Father is asked (v. 14) to strengthen the believers through His Spirit (v. 16) that Christ might be completely at home in their hearts (v. 17). One of the great privileges of prayer is that we can engage the eternal Godhead to work in behalf of others and of ourselves.

The result of Christ's unrestricted access is that the Christian becomes rooted and grounded in love. Here Paul borrows words from the worlds of botany and of building. The root of a plant provides nourishment and support. The groundwork of a building is the foundation on which it rests. "Love is the soil in which our life must have its roots; and it is the rock upon which our faith must ever rest" (Scroggie). To be rooted and grounded in love is to be established in love as a way of life. The life of love is a life of kindness, selflessness, brokenness and meekness. It is the life of Christ finding expression in the believer (see I Cor. 13:4-7).

3:18 The preceding requests have outlined a program of spiritual growth and development which prepares the child of God to be fully able to grasp "with all saints what is the breadth, and length, and depth, and height."

Before we consider the dimensions themselves, let us notice the expression "with all saints." The subject is so great that no one believer can possibly grasp more than a small fraction of it. So there is need to study, discuss and share with others. The Holy Spirit can use the combined meditations of a group of exercised believers to throw a flood of additional light on the Scriptures.

The dimensions are generally taken to refer to the love of Christ, although the text does not say this. In fact, the love of Christ is mentioned separately in the following clause. If the love of Christ is intended, then the connection might be shown as follows:

Breadth——The world (John 3:16)
Length——Forever (I Cor. 13:8)
Depth——Even the death of the cross (Phil. 2:8)
Height——Heaven (I John 3:1-2)

"There will always be as much horizon before us as behind us. And when we have been gazing on the face of Jesus for millenniums, its beauty will be as fresh and fascinating and fathomless as when we first saw it from the gate of Paradise" (F. B. Meyer).

But these dimensions may also refer to the mystery which holds such an important place in the epistle. In fact, it is easy to find these dimensions in the text of the epistle itself:

1. The breadth is described in 2:11-18. It refers to the wideness of God's grace in saving Jews and Gentiles, and then incorporating them into the church. The mystery embraces both these segments of humanity.

2. The length extends from eternity to eternity. As to the past, believers were chosen in Christ before the foundation of the world (1:4). As to the future, eternity will be a perpetual unfolding of the exceeding riches of His grace in His kindness toward us through Christ Jesus (2:7).

3. The depth is vividly portrayed in 2:1-3. We were sunk in a pit of unspeakable sin and degradation. Christ came to this jungle of filth and corruption in order to die in our behalf.

4. The height is seen in 2:6, where we have not only been raised up with Christ, but enthroned in Him in the heavenlies to share His glory.

These are the dimensions, then, of immensity and indeed, of infinity. As we think of them, "all we can do is to mark the order in this tumult of holy words" (Scroggie).

3:19 The apostle's next request is that the saints might know by experience the knowledge-surpassing love of Christ. They could never explore it fully because it is an ocean without shores, but they could learn more and more about it from day to day. And so he prays for a deep, experimental knowledge and enjoyment of the wonderful love of our wonderful Lord.

The climax in this magnificent prayer is reached when Paul prays "that ye may be filled unto all the fulness of God" (ASV). All the fullness of the Godhead dwells in the Lord Jesus (Col. 2:9). The more He dwells in our hearts by faith, the more we are filled unto all the fullness of God.

We could never be filled *with* all the fullness of God. But it is a goal *unto* which we move.

And yet having explained this, we must say that there are depths of meaning here that we have not reached. As we handle the Scriptures, we are aware that we are dealing with truths that are greater than our ability to understand or explain. We can use illustrations to throw light on this verse, for example, the thimble dipped in the ocean is filled with water, but how little of the ocean is in the thimble. Yet when we have said all this, the mystery remains, and we can only stand in awe at God's Word and marvel at its infinity.

VIII. Paul's Praise to God (3:20-21)

    A. The Praise-worthy One (v. 20): *Now unto him* (God)

    B. His Ability (v. 20): *who is able to do*

    C. The Extent of His Ability (v. 20): *exceeding abundantly above all we ask or think*

    D. The Power He Uses (v. 20): *according to the power that worketh in us*

    E. The Praise Due Him (v. 21): *to him be glory* (RSV)

    F. The Source of This Praise (v. 21): *in the church and in Christ Jesus* (RSV)

    G. The Duration of This Praise (v. 21): *to all generations, for ever and ever* (RSV)

    H. The Heart's Response (v. 21): *Amen*

3:20 The prayer closes with a soul-inspiring doxology. The preceding requests have been vast, bold and seemingly impossible. But God is able to do more in this connection than we can ask or think.

The extent of His ability is seen in the manner in which Paul pyramids words to describe superabundant blessings:

Able

Able to do

Able to do what we ask

Able to do what we think

Able to do what we ask or think

Able to do all that we ask or think

Able to do above all that we ask or think

Able to do abundantly above all that we ask or think

Able to do exceeding abundantly above all that we ask or think

The means by which God answers prayer is given in the expression "according to the power that worketh in us." This refers to the Holy Spirit who is constantly at work in our lives, seeking to produce the fruit of a Christlike character, reproving us of sin, guiding us in prayer, inspiring us in worship, directing us in service. The more we are yielded to Him, the greater will be His effectiveness in conforming us to Christ.

3:21 "Unto Him be the glory in the church and in Christ Jesus unto all generations for ever and ever. Amen" (ASV).

God is the worthy object of eternal praise. His wisdom and His power are displayed in the angelic hosts, in sun, moon and stars, in animals, birds and fish, in fire, hail, snow and mist, in wind, in mountains, hills, trees, in kings and people, old men and young, in Israel and the nations; all these are intended to praise the name of the Lord (Ps. 148).

But there is another group from which endless glory will be given to God, that is, from the church—from Christ the Head and from believers, the body. This redeemed community will be an eternal witness to His matchless, marvelous grace. "The eternal glory of God as God and Father will be made visible throughout all ages in the Church and in Christ Jesus. Amazing statement! Christ and the Church as One Body will be the vehicle of that eternal demonstration" (Williams).

Even now the church should be giving glory to His name "in the services of praise, in the pure lives of its members, in its world-wide proclamation of the Gospel, and in its ministries to human distress and need" (Erdman).

The duration of this praise is "unto all generations for ever and ever." As we hear Paul call for eternal praise to God in the church and in Christ Jesus, the response of our hearts is a hearty AMEN!

4

IX. Exhortations to a Worthy Walk (4:1–6:9)

    A. Appeal for Unity in the Christian Fellowship (vv. 1-6)

        1. The author (v. 1): *I therefore, the prisoner of the Lord*

        2. The general appeal (v. 1): *beseech you that ye walk worthy*

        3. The standard (v. 1): *of the vocation wherewith ye are called*

        4. The attitude (v. 2): *With all lowliness and meekness, with longsuffering, forbearing one another in love*

        5. The specific aim (v. 3): *Endeavoring to keep the unity of the Spirit in the bond of peace*

        6. The sevenfold basis of unity (vv. 4-6): *There is one body, and one Spirit, even as ye are called in one hope of your calling; one Lord, one faith, one baptism, one God and Father of all, who is above all, and through all, and in you all*

4:1 There is a distinct break at this point in the epistle. The previous chapters have dealt with the Christian's calling. In the last three chapters, he is urged to walk worthy of his calling. The position into which grace has lifted us was the dominant theme up to now. From here on, it will be the practical outworking of that position. Our exalted standing in Christ calls for corresponding godly conduct. So it is true that Ephesians moves from the heavenlies in chapters 1–3, to the local church, to the home, and to general society in chapters 4–6.

For the second time Paul refers to himself as a prisoner—this time as a prisoner in the Lord. Theodoret comments: "What the world counted ignominy, he counts the highest honor, and he glories in his bonds for Christ, more than a king in his diadem."

As one who was imprisoned as a result of faithfulness and obedience to the Lord, the apostle exhorts his readers to walk worthily of their calling. He does not command or direct. With tenderness and gentleness he appeals to them in the language of grace.

The word "walk" is found seven times in this letter (2:2, 10; 4:1, 17; 5:2, 8, 15); it describes a person's entire behavior cycle. A worthy walk is one that is consistent with a Christian's dignified position as a member of the body of Christ.

4:2 In every sphere of life, it is important to manifest a Christlike spirit. This consists of:

Lowliness—a genuine humility that comes from association with the Lord Jesus. Lowliness makes us conscious of our own nothingness and enables us to esteem others better than ourselves. It is the opposite of conceit and arrogance.

Meekness—the attitude that submits to God's dealings without rebellion, and to man's unkindness without retaliation. It is best seen in the life of Him who said, "I am meek and lowly in heart." "What an astonishingly wonderful statement! The One who made the worlds, Who flung the stars into space and calls them by name, Who preserves the innumerable constellations in their courses, Who weighs the mountains in scales and the hills in a balance, Who takes up the isles as a very little thing, Who holds the water of the ocean in the hollow of His hand, before Whom the inhabitants of the world are as grasshoppers, when He comes into human life finds Himself as essentially meek and lowly in heart. It is not that He erected a perfect human ideal and accommodated Himself to it; He was that" (Wright).

Longsuffering—an even disposition and a spirit of patience under prolonged provocation. This has been illustrated as follows: Imagine a puppy and a big dog together. As the puppy barks at the big dog, worrying and attacking him, the big dog, who could snap up the puppy with one bite, patiently puts up with the puppy's impertinence.

Forbearing one another in love—that is, making allowance for the faults and failures of others, for differing personalities, abilities and temperaments. And it is not a question of maintaining a facade of courtesy while inwardly seething with resentment. It means positive love to those who irritate, disturb or embarrass.

4:3 "Giving diligence to keep the unity of the Spirit in the bond of peace." In forming the church, God had eliminated the greatest division that had ever existed among human beings—the rift between Jews and Gentiles. In Christ Jesus these distinctions were abolished. But how would it work out in their life together? Would there still be lingering antagonisms? Would there be a tendency to form a "Jewish Church of Christ" and a "Church for the Nations"? To guard against any divisions or smoldering animosities, Paul now pleads for unity among Christians.

They should give diligence to keep the unity of the Spirit. The Holy Spirit has made all true believers one in Christ; the body is indwelt by one Spirit. This is a basic unity that nothing can destroy. But by quarreling and bickering, believers can act as if it were not so. To keep the unity of the Spirit means to live at peace with one another. Peace is the ligament which binds the members of the body together in spite of their wide natural differences.

The natural reaction when differences arise is to divide and start another party. The spiritual reaction is this: "In essentials, unity. In doubtful questions, liberty. In all things, charity."

There is enough of the flesh in every one of us to wreck any local church or any other work of God. Therefore, we must submerge our own petty, personal whims and attitudes, and work together in peace for the glory of God and for common blessing.

4:4 Instead of magnifying differences, we should think of the seven positive realities which form the basis of true Christian unity.

One body. In spite of differences in race, color, nationality, culture, language and temperament, yet there is only one body, made up of all true believers from Pentecost to the rapture. Denominations, sects and parties hinder the outworking of this truth. All such man-made divisions will be swept away when the Savior returns. Therefore, our watchword at the present time should be, "Let names and sects and parties fall, and Jesus Christ be all in all."

One Spirit. The same Holy Spirit who indwells each believer individually (I Cor. 6:19) also indwells the body of Christ (I Cor. 3:16).

One hope. Every member of the church is called to one destiny—to be with Christ, to be like Him and to share His glory endlessly. The one hope includes all that awaits the saints at the return of the Lord Jesus and thereafter.

4:5 *One Lord.* "For although there may be so-called gods in heaven or on earth—as indeed there are many 'gods' and many 'lords'—yet for us there is one God, . . . and one Lord, Jesus Christ, through whom are all things and through whom we exist" (I Cor. 8:5-6, RSV). (See also I Cor. 1:2.)

One faith. This is the Christian faith, the body of doctrine "once for all delivered unto the saints" (Jude 3, RV), and preserved for us in the New Testament.

One baptism. There is a twofold sense in which this is true. First of all, there is one baptism by the Spirit by which those who trust Christ are placed in the body (I

Cor. 12:13). Then there is one baptism by which converts confess their identification with Christ in death, burial and resurrection. Though there are different modes of baptism today, the New Testament recognizes one believers' baptism, in the name of the Father and of the Son and of the Holy Spirit. By being baptized, disciples express allegiance to Christ, the burial of their old self, and a determination to walk in newness of life.

4:6 *One God.* Every child of God recognizes one God and one Father of all the redeemed who is:

> *Over all*—He is the supreme Sovereign of the universe.

> *Through all*—He acts through all, using everything to accomplish His purposes.

> *In all*—He dwells in all believers, and is present in all places at one and the same time.

B. Program for the Proper Functioning of the Members of the Body (vv. 7-16)
  1. A role assigned to each believer (v. 7)
      a. Individual importance: *But to every one of us*
      b. Specific function: *is given grace*
      c. Sovereign variety: *according to the measure of the gift of Christ*
  2. Special service gifts for the growth of the church (vv. 8-16)
      a. The Giver of the gifts—the ascended Christ (vv. 8-10)
        1) Christ's ascension predicted in Psalm 68:18 (v. 8): *Wherefore he saith, when he ascended up on high, he led captivity captive, and gave gifts unto men.*
        2) His ascension implies a prior descent to the earth (v. 9): *Now that he ascended, what is it but that he also descended first into the lower parts of the earth?*

> 3) His descent in incarnation was followed by ascension and glory (v. 10): *He that descended is the same also that ascended up far above all heavens, that he might fill all things*

b. The names of the gifts (v. 11): *And he gave some [to be], apostles; and some, prophets; and some, evangelists; and some, pastors and teachers*

c. The function of the gifts (v. 12)
  1) The gifts equip the saints: *For the perfecting of the saints*
  2) The saints then serve: *unto the work of the ministry* (FWG)
  3) The body is then built up: *unto the edifying of the body of Christ* (FWG)

d. The duration of the growth process (v. 13)
  1) Unity: *Till we all come in the unity of the faith, and of the knowledge of the Son of God*
  2) Maturity: *to mature manhood* (RSV)
  3) Conformity: *unto the measure of the stature of the fulness of Christ*

e. Dangers avoided by the proper functioning of the gifts (v. 14)
  1) Immaturity: *That we henceforth be no more children*
  2) Instability: *tossed to and fro*
  3) Gullibility: *and carried about with every wind of doctrine, by the sleight of men, and cunning craftiness, whereby they lie in wait to deceive*

f. The proper process of growth in the body (vv. 15-16)
  1) The necessity of doctrinal adherence (v. 15): *but, holding the truth* (JND)
  2) The necessity of a right spirit (v. 15): *in love*
  3) The aim or object of growth (v. 15): *may grow up into him*
  4) The areas of growth (v. 15): *in all things*
  5) The Head of the body (v. 15): *which is the head, even Christ*
  6) The Source of growth (v. 16): *From whom [Christ]*

7) The integration of the members of the body
(v. 16): *the whole body fitly joined together
and compacted*

8) The function of each member (v. 16): *by
that which every joint supplieth*

9) The necessity of each member's fulfilling his
function (v. 16): *according to the effectual
working in the measure of every part*

10) The growth that results (v. 16): *maketh increase
of the body*

11) The mutual concern of the members (v. 16):
unto the edifying of itself in love

4:7   The truth of the unity of the body of Christ has a twin
truth, namely, the diversity of its members. Each member
has a particular role assigned. No two members are alike and
no two have exactly the same function. The part to be played
by each one is assigned according to the measure of the gift
of Christ, that is, He does it as He sees fit. If the gift of Christ
here means the Holy Spirit (John 14:16-17; Acts 2:38-39),
then the thought is that the Holy Spirit is the One who assigns
some gift to every saint, and who also gives the ability
to exercise that gift. As each member fulfills his appointed
work, the body of Christ grows both spiritually and numerically.

4:8   In order to assist each child of God to find his function
and to fulfill it, the Lord has given some special gifts
of ministry, or service to the church. These should not be
confused with the gifts mentioned in the previous verse.
Every believer has some gift (v. 7), but not everyone is one
of the gifts named in verse 11; these are special gifts designed
for the growth of the body.

First of all, we find that the Giver of those special gifts of
ministry is the risen, ascended, glorified Lord Jesus Christ.
Paul quotes Psalm 68:18 as a prophecy that the Messiah
would ascend to heaven, that He would conquer His foes
and lead them captive and, as a reward for His victory, He
would receive gifts for men.

4:9 But this raises a problem! How could the Messiah ascend to heaven? Had He not lived in heaven with God the Father from all eternity? Obviously, if He was to ascend to heaven, He must first come down from heaven. The prophecy of His ascension in Psalm 68:18 implies a prior descent. So we might paraphrase verse 9 as follows: "Now when it says in Psalm 68 'He ascended' what can it mean but that He first descended to the lower parts of the earth." We know that this is exactly what happened. The Lord Jesus descended to Bethlehem's manger, to the death of the cross, and to the grave.

"The lower parts of the earth" have sometimes been taken to refer to hades or hell. But that would not fit in with the argument here: His ascension necessitated a previous descent to earth but not to hell. In addition, the Scriptures indicate that Christ's spirit went to heaven, not hell when He died (Luke 23:43, 46).

The New English Bible translates this verse: "Now the word 'ascended' implies that he also descended to the lowest level, down to the very earth."

4:10 The prophecy of Psalm 68:18 and the descent implied in the prophecy were exactly fulfilled by the incarnation, death and burial of the Lord Jesus. The One who descended from heaven is the same One who conquered sin, Satan, demons, and death, and who ascended above the atmosphere and stellar heavens that He might fill all things.

He fills all things in the sense that He is the source of all blessing, the sum of all virtues and the supreme Sovereign over all. "There is not a place between the depth of the Cross and the height of the glory which He has not occupied" (F. W. Grant).

The central thought in verses 8-10 is that the Giver of the gifts is the ascended Christ. There were no such gifts before He went back to heaven. This lends further support to the contention that the church did not exist in the Old Testament; for if it did, it was a church without gifts.

4:11 The names of the gifts are now given. To our surprise we find that they are men, not natural endowments or talents. "He gave some to be apostles; and some, prophets; and some, evangelists; and some, pastors and teachers" (RV).

Apostles were men who were directly commissioned by the Lord to preach the Word and to plant churches. They were men who had seen Christ in resurrection (Acts 1:22). They had power to perform miracles (II Cor. 12:12) as a means of confirming the message they preached (Heb. 2:4). Together with New Testament prophets, their ministry was primarily concerned with the foundation of the church (Eph. 2:20). The apostles referred to in this passage mean only those who were apostles *after* the ascension of Christ.

Prophets were spokesmen or mouthpieces of God. They received direct revelations from the Lord and passed them on to the church. What they spoke by the Holy Spirit was the Word of God.

In the primary sense we no longer have apostles and prophets. Their ministry was ended when the foundation of the church was laid, and when the New Testament canon was completed.

We have already emphasized that Paul is speaking here of New Testament prophets; they were given by Christ after His ascension. To think of them as Old Testament prophets introduces difficulties and absurdities into the passage.

Evangelists are those who preach the good news of salvation. They are divinely equipped to win the lost to Christ. They have special ability to diagnose a sinner's condition, to probe the conscience, to answer objections, to encourage decisions for Christ and to help the convert find assurance through the Word.

Evangelists should go out from a local church, preach to the world, then lead their converts to a local church where they will be fed and encouraged.

Pastors are men who serve as under-shepherds of the sheep of Christ. They guide and feed the flock. Theirs is a ministry of wise counsel, correction, encouragement and consolation.

The work of pastors is closely related to that of elders in a local church, the principal difference being that a pastor is a gift whereas the elder is not.

The New Testament pictures several pastors in a local church (Acts 20:17, 28; I Peter 5:1-2) rather than one pastor or presiding elder.

Teachers are men who are divinely empowered to explain what the Bible says, to interpret what it means and to apply it to the hearts and consciences of the saints. Whereas an evangelist may preach the gospel from a passage out of context, the teacher seeks to show how the passage fits into the context.

Because pastors and teachers are linked in this verse, some conclude that only one gift is intended, that it should read "pastor-teachers." But this is not necessarily so. A man may be a teacher without having the heart of a shepherd. And a pastor may be able to use the Word without having the distinctive gift of teaching. If pastors and teachers are the same persons here in verse 11, then, by the same rule of grammar, so are apostles and prophets in 2:20.

One final word. We should be careful to distinguish between divine gifts and natural talents. No unsaved person, however talented, could be an evangelist, pastor or teacher in the New Testament sense. Neither could a Christian, for that matter, unless he has received that particular gift. The gifts of the Spirit are supernatural. They enable a man to do what would be humanly impossible for him.

4:12 We come now to the function or purpose of the gifts. It is "for the perfecting of the saints unto the work of the ministry, unto the edifying of the body of Christ" (FWG). As indicated in the outline, the process is this:

1. The gifts equip the saints.
2. The saints then serve.
3. The body is then built up.

The ministry is not a specialized occupation limited to men with professional training. The word simply means *service*.

It includes every form of spiritual service. And what this verse teaches is that every believer should be "in the ministry."

The gifts are given to perfect or equip all Christians to serve the Lord, and thus to build up the body of Christ.

"Every Christian is commissioned, for every Christian is a missionary. It has been said that the Gospel is not merely something to come to church to hear but something to go from church to tell—and we are all appointed to tell it. It has also been said, 'Christianity began as a company of lay witnesses; it has become a professional pulpitism, financed by lay spectators!' Nowadays we hire a church staff to do 'full-time Christian work,' and we sit in church on Sunday to watch them do it. Every Christian is meant to be in full-time Christian service. . . . There is indeed a special ministry of pastors, teachers and evangelists—but for what? . . . For the perfecting of the saints for their ministry" (Vance Havner).

These divinely given men should not serve in such a way as to make people perpetually dependent on them. Instead, they should work toward the day when the saints will be able to carry on by themselves. We might illustrate this as follows:

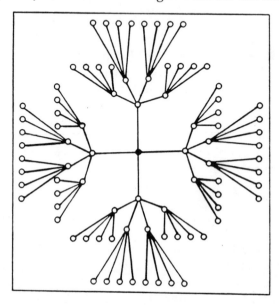

The circle in the center depicts, let us say, the gift of a teacher. He ministers to those in the circle around him, so that they become perfected, that is, built up in the faith. Then they go forth and minister to others according to the gifts God has given them. In this way the church grows and expands. It is the divine method of producing growth in the body of Christ, both in size and in spirituality.

Limitation of Christian service to a select class of men hinders the development of God's people, stifles the cause of world evangelism and stunts the growth of the church. The distinction between clergy and laity is unscriptural and is perhaps the greatest single hindrance to the spread of the gospel.

4:13 Verse 13 answers the question "How long will this growth process continue?" The answer is until we all come to unity, maturity and conformity.

Unity. When the Lord takes His church home to heaven, we will all arrive at the unity of the faith. "Now we see through a glass darkly" with regard to many matters. We have differences of opinion on a host of subjects. Then we will all be fully agreed.

And we will reach the unity of the knowledge of the Son of God. Here we have individual views of the Lord, of what He is like, of the implications of His teachings. Then we will see Him as He is, and know as we are known.

Maturity. At the rapture we will also reach full growth or maturity. Both as individuals and as the body of Christ, we will achieve perfection of spiritual development.

Conformity. And we will be conformed to Him. Everyone will be morally like the Lord Jesus. And the universal church will be a full-grown body, perfectly suited to its glorious Head. "The fulness of Christ is the Church itself, the fulness of Him that filleth all in all" (FWG). The measure of the stature of the church means its complete development, the fulfillment of God's plan for its growth.

4:14 When the gifts operate in their God-appointed manner and the saints are active in service for the Lord, three dangers are avoided—immaturity, instability and gullibility.

Immaturity. Believers who never become involved in aggressive service for Christ never emerge from spiritual childhood. They remain undeveloped through lack of exercise. It was to such that the writer to the Hebrews said, "For when by reason of the time ye ought to be teachers, ye have need again that some one teach you. . . ." (Heb. 5:12, RV).

Instability. Another danger is spiritual fickleness. Immature Christians are susceptible to the grotesque novelties and fads of professional quacks. They become religious gypsies, moving about from one appealing fantasy to another.

Gullibility. Most serious of all is the danger of deception. Those who are babes are unskillful in the word of righteousness, their senses are not exercised to discern between good and evil (Heb. 5:13-14, RV). They inevitably meet some false cultist who impresses them by his zeal and apparent sincerity. Because he uses religious words, they think he must be a true Christian. If they had studied the Bible for themselves, they would be able to see through his deceitful juggling of words. But now they are carried about by his winds of doctrine and led by unprincipled cunning into a form of systematized error.

4:15 The last two verses in the paragraph describe the proper process of growth in the body of Christ.

First of all, there is the necessity of doctrinal adherence: "But, holding the truth. . . ." (JND). There can be no compromise as to the fundamentals of the faith.

Second, there must be a right spirit: "But holding the truth in love" (JND). If it is held in any other way, the result is a one-sided testimony. "Truth is the element in which we are to live, move and have our being. . . . But truth must be inseparably married to love; good tidings spoken harshly are no good tidings. The charm of the message is destroyed by the discordant spirit of the messenger" (Pulpit Commentary).

Then as the gifts equip the saints, and as the saints engage in active service, they grow up into Christ in all things. Christ is the aim and object of their growth, and the sphere of growth is "in all things." In every area of their lives they become more like Him.

As the Head has His way in the church, His body will give an ever more accurate representation of Him to the world!

4:16 The Lord Jesus is not only the goal of growth, He is the source of growth as well. From Him, "the whole Body . . . maketh increase of the Body."

The marvelous integration of the members of the body is described by the phrase "fitly joined together." This means that every member is exactly designed for his own place and function, and perfectly joined to every other member so as to make a complete, living organism.

The importance, yes, the indispensability of every member is next indicated: "compacted by that which every joint supplieth." The human body consists primarily of bones, organs and flesh. The bones are bound together by joints and ligaments, and the organs also are attached by ligaments. Each joint and ligament fulfills a role in the growth and usefulness of the body. So it is in the body of Christ. No member is superficial; even the most humble believer is necessary.

As each believer fulfills his proper role, the body grows as an harmonious, well-articulated unit. In a very real sense, the body makes increase of the body, paradoxical as it sounds. This simply means that growth is stimulated by the body itself as the members feed on the Bible, spend time in prayer, in worship and witness for Christ. "The Church, like the human body, is self-developing" (Chafer).

In addition to growth in size, there is a building up of

itself in love. This speaks of the mutual concern of the members for one another. As Christians abide in Christ and fulfill their proper function in the church, they grow closer to one another in love and unity.

C. Appeal for a New Morality (4:17–5:21)

    1. The pagan life to be discarded (4:17-19): *Now this I affirm and testify in the Lord, that you must no longer live as the Gentiles do* (RSV)

        a. Aimless (v. 17): *in the vanity of their mind*

        b. Blind (v. 18): *having the understanding darkened*

        c. Ungodly (v. 18): *being alienated from the life of God*

            1) Ignorant: *through the ignorance that is in them*

            2) Callous: *due to their hardness of heart* (RSV)

        d. Shameless (v. 19): *Who being past feeling*

        e. Abandoned (v. 19): *have given themselves over to lasciviousness*

        f. Sordid (v. 19): *to work all uncleanness*

        g. Insatiable (v. 19): *with greediness*

    2. The Christian life to be followed (4:20-24)

        a. Its sharp contrast to the pagan life (v. 20): *But ye have not so learned Christ*

        b. The Teacher of the new walk (v. 21): *If so be that ye have heard him, and have been taught by him*

        c. The embodiment of the truth (v. 21): *as the truth is in Jesus*

        d. The lessons taught (vv. 22-24)

            1) The old man put off (v. 22): *That ye have put away as concerning your former manner of life the old man, which corrupteth itself according to the deceitful lusts* (FWG)

            2) The spirit of the mind being renewed (v. 23): *and that ye are being renewed in the spirit of your mind* (FWG)

            3) The new man put on (v. 24): *and that ye have put on the new man* (FWG)

> a) His likeness: *which after God*
> b) His character: *is created in righteousness and holiness of truth* (FWG)

4:17 This verse begins the apostle's eloquent appeal for a new morality, an appeal which extends to 5:21. Testifying in the Lord, that is, by authority of the Lord and by divine inspiration, he urges the Christians to put off every trace of their past life, as if it were a muddy coat, and to put on the virtues and excellencies of the Lord Jesus Christ.

"You must no longer live as the Gentiles do" (RSV). They were no longer Gentiles; they were Christians. There should be a corresponding change in their lives.

Paul saw the Christless world of the nations sunk in ignorance and degradation. Seven terrible things characterized them. They were:

Aimless. They walked in the vanity of their minds. Their life was empty, purposeless and fruitless. There was great activity but no progress. They chased bubbles and shadows, and neglected the great realities of life.

4:18 *Blind.* "They live blindfold in a world of illusion" (JBP). Their understandings were darkened. First of all, they had a native incapacity to understand spiritual truths, and then, because of their rejection of the knowledge of the true God, they suffered blindness as a judgment from the Lord.

Ungodly. They were alienated from the life of God, or at a great distance from Him. This was brought about by their willful, deep-seated ignorance and by the hardness of their hearts. They had rejected the light of God in creation and in conscience, and had turned to idolatry. Thereafter they had plunged farther and farther from God.

4:19 *Shameless.* They were past feeling. "Moule translates it: 'having got over the pain.' How expressive! When conscience is at first denied, there is a twinge of pain; there is a protest that can be heard. But if the

voice is silenced, presently the voice becomes less clear
and clamant; the protest is smothered; the twinge is less
acute, until at last it is possible to 'get over the pain.' "
(W. C. Wright).

Sordid. They consciously gave themselves over to lascivi-
ousness, that is, to vile forms of behavior. The cardinal
sin of the Gentiles was and still is sexual immorality.
They descended to unparalleled depths of depravity;
the walls of Pompeii tell the story of shame and lost de-
cency. The same sins characterize the Gentile world
today.

Indecent. In their sexual sin, they worked all uncleanness.
There is a suggestion here that they gave themselves
up to every kind of uncleanness as if they were carrying on a trade or business in lewdness.

Insatiable. "With greediness." They were never satisfied.
They never had enough. Their sin created an enormous
appetite for more of the same thing.

4:20 How different all this was from the Christ whom the
Ephesians had come to know and love! He was the personification of purity and chastity. He knew no sin, He did no
sin, there was no sin in Him.

4:21 The "if" here ("if so be that ye have heard him") is
not meant to cast doubt on the conversion of the Ephesians.
It simply emphasizes that all those who had heard Christ
and had been taught in Him had come to know Him as the
essence of holiness and godliness. To have heard Christ
means to have heard Him with the hearing of faith—to have
accepted Him as Lord and Savior. The expression "taught
in him" (ASV) refers to the instruction the Ephesians received as they walked in fellowship with Him subsequent
to their conversion. "All truth acquires a different hue and a
different character when there is a personal relation to Jesus.
Truth apart from the Person of Christ has little power"
(Pulpit Commentary).

"Even as truth is in Jesus" (RV). He not only teaches the truth; He is truth incarnate (John 14:6). The name Jesus here takes us back to His life on earth, since that is His name in incarnation. In that spotless life which He lived as a Man in this world, we see the very antithesis of the walk of the Gentiles which Paul has just described.

4:22   In the school of Christ, we learn that at the time of conversion we put away our old man which is corrupt through deceitful lusts. The old man means all that a person was before his conversion, all that he was as a child of Adam. It is corrupted as a result of giving in to deceitful, evil cravings which are pleasant and promising in anticipation but hideous and disappointing in retrospect.

As far as his position in Christ is concerned, the believer's old man was crucified with Christ and buried with Him. In practice, the believer should reckon it to be dead. Here Paul is emphasizing the positional side of the truth—we have put off the old man once for all.

4:23   A second lesson the Ephesians learned at the feet of Jesus was that they were being renewed in the spirit of their mind. This points to a complete about-face in their thinking, a change from mental impurity to holiness. The Spirit of God influences the thought processes to reason from God's standpoint, not from that of unsaved men.

4:24   The third lesson is that they had put the new man on once for all. The new man is what a believer is in Christ. It is the new creation, in which old things have passed away and all things have become new (II Cor. 5:17).

This new kind of man is "after God," that is, created in the likeness of God. And it manifests itself in righteousness and holiness of truth. Righteousness means right conduct toward others. "Holiness is the piety which puts God in His true place" (FWG).

3. Lying and truthfulness (4:25)
    a. Negative: *Wherefore putting away lying*
    b. Positive: *speak every man truth with his neighbour*
    c. Motive: *for we are members one of another*

4. Sinful wrath and righteous anger (4:26-27)
    a. Admonition (v. 26): *Be ye angry*
    b. Prohibition (v. 26): *and sin not*
    c. Limitation (v. 26): *let not the sun go down upon your wrath*
    d. Occasion (v. 27): *Neither give place [occasion] to the devil.*

5. Stealing and sharing (4:28)
    a. Former thief: *Let him that stole*
    b. New leaf: *steal no more:*
    c. Hard worker: *but rather let him labour*
    d. No shirker: *working with his hands*
    e. Honest occupation: *the thing which is good*
    f. Highest motivation: *that he may have to give to him that needeth*

6. Corrupt chatter and speech that edifies (4:29-30)
    a. Taboo talk (v. 29): *Let no corrupt communication proceed out of your mouth*
    b. Constructive conversation (v. 29)
        1) Edifying: *but only such as is good for edifying* (RSV)
        2) Appropriate: *as fits the occasion* (RSV)
        3) Gracious: *that it may impart grace to those who hear* (RSV)
    c. Tongue test (v. 30): *And grieve not the holy Spirit of God, whereby ye are sealed unto the day of redemption*

7. Hot heads and tender hearts (4:31-32)
    a. Sins of temper to terminate (v. 31): *Let all bitterness, and wrath, and anger, and clamour and evil speaking, be put away from you, with all malice*
    b. Christlike virtues to cultivate (v. 32)
        1) Kindness: *And be ye kind one to another*

    2) Tenderness: *tenderhearted*
    3) Forgiveness: *forgiving one another*
       a) The great Example: *even as God*
       b) The basis of His forgiveness: *in Christ* (RSV)
       c) The unworthy objects: *hath forgiven you*

4:25 The apostle now moves from the believers' standing to their state. Because they have put off the old man and have put on the new man through their union with Christ, they should demonstrate this startling reversal in their everyday lives.

They can do this, first of all, by putting off lying and putting on truthfulness. Lying here includes every form of dishonesty, whether it is shading of the truth, exaggeration, cheating, failure to keep promises, betrayal of confidence, flattery or fudging on income taxes.

The Christian's word should be absolutely trustworthy. His yes should mean yes, and his no, no. The life of a Christian becomes a libel rather than a Bible when he stoops to any form of tampering with truthfulness.

Truth is a debt we owe to all men. However, when Paul uses the word "neighbour" here, he is thinking particularly of our fellow believers. This is clear from the motive given: "for we are members one of another." (Cf. Rom. 12:5; I Cor. 12:12-27.) It is as unthinkable for one Christian to lie to another as it would be for a nerve in the body to deliberately send a false message to the brain, or for the eye to deceive the rest of the body when danger is approaching.

4:26 A second area for practical renewal in our lives is in connection with sinful wrath and righteous anger.

There are times when a believer may be righteously angry, for instance, when the character of God is impugned. In such cases, anger is commanded: "Be ye angry, . . ." Anger against evil can be righteous.

But there are other times when anger is sinful. When it is an emotion of malice, jealousy, resentment, vindictiveness or hatred because of personal wrongs, it is forbidden.

If a believer gives way to unrighteous wrath, he should confess and forsake it quickly. Confession should be made both to God and to the victim of his anger. There should be no nursing of grudges, no harboring of resentments, no carrying over of irritations. "Let not the sun go down on your wrath." Anything that mars fellowship with God or with our brethren should immediately be made right.

4:27 Unconfessed sins of temper provide the devil with a foothold or a base of operations. He is capable of finding plenty of these without our deliberately helping him. Therefore, we must not excuse malice, wrath, envy, hatred or passion in our lives. These sins discredit the Christian testimony, stumble the unsaved, offend believers, and harm ourselves spiritually and physically.

4:28 Now Paul turns his attention to the contrasting behavior patterns of stealing and sharing. The old man steals; the new man shares. Put off the old; put on the new!

The fact that Paul would ever address such instruction to believers ("Let him that stole steal no more") disproves any notion that Christians are sinlessly perfect. They still have the old, evil, selfish nature that must be reckoned dead in daily experience.

Stealing may take many forms—all the way from grand larceny to nonpayment of debts, to witnessing for Christ on the employer's time, to plagiarism, to the use of false measurements, and to falsifying expense accounts.

Of course, this prohibition against stealing is not new. The law of Moses forbade theft (Exodus 20:15). It is what follows that makes the passage distinctively Christian. Not only should we refrain from stealing, we should actually work diligently in an honorable occupation in order to be able to share with others who are less fortunate. Grace, not law, is the power of holiness. Only the positive power of grace can turn a thief into a philanthropist.

This is radical and revolutionary. The natural approach is for men to work for the supply of their own needs and desires. When their income rises, their standard of living rises. Everything in their lives revolves around self. This verse suggests a nobler, more exalted view of secular employment. It is a means of supplying a modest standard of living for one's family, but also of alleviating human need, spiritual and temporal, at home and abroad. And how vast that need is!

4:29 The apostle now turns to the subject of speech, and contrasts that which is worthless with that which edifies. Corrupt communications generally mean conversation that is filthy and suggestive; this would include off-color jokes, profanity and dirty stories.

But here it probably has the wider sense of any form of conversation that is frivolous, empty, idle and worthless. The apostle deals with obscene and vile language in 5:4; here he is telling us to abandon profitless speech and substitute constructive conversation. The Christian's speech should be:

Edifying. It should result in building up the hearers.

Appropriate. It should be "as fits the occasion" (RSV).

Gracious. It should impart grace to those who hear.

4:30 "And grieve not the holy Spirit of God, whereby ye are sealed unto the day of redemption." If this is taken in connection with the preceding verse, it means that worthless talk grieves the Spirit. It may also be linked to verses 25-28 to indicate that lying, unrighteous anger and stealing also hurt Him. Or in a still wider sense, it may be saying that we should abstain from anything and everything that grieves Him.

Three powerful reasons are suggested:

1. He is the *Holy* Spirit. Anything that is not holy is distasteful to Him.
2. He is the Holy Spirit of *God,* a member of the blessed Trinity.
3. We are sealed by Him unto the day of redemption. As mentioned previously, a seal speaks of ownership and security. He is the seal that guarantees our preserva-

tion until Christ returns for us and our salvation is complete. Interestingly enough, Paul here uses the eternal security of the believer as one of the strongest reasons why we should *not* sin.

The fact that He can be grieved shows that the Holy Spirit is a Person, not a mere influence. It also means that He loves us, because only a person who loves can be grieved.

The favorite ministry of God's Spirit is to glorify Christ and to change the believer into His likeness (II Cor. 3:18). When a Christian sins, He has to turn from this ministry to one of restoration. It grieves Him to see the believers' spiritual progress interrupted by sin. He must then lead the Christian to the place of repentance and confession of sin.

4:31 All sins of temper and of tongue should be put away. The apostle lists several of them. Though it is not possible to distinguish each one precisely, the overall meaning is clear:

Bitterness—Smouldering resentment, unwillingness to forgive, harsh feeling.

Wrath—Bursts of rage, violent passion, temper tantrums.

Anger—Grouchiness, animosity, hostility.

Clamor—Loud outcries of anger, brawling, angry bickering, shouting down of opponents.

Railing—Insulting language, slander, abusive speech.

Malice—Wishing evil on others, spite, meanness.

4:32 The foregoing sins of temper should be terminated, but the vacuum must be filled by the cultivation of Christlike qualities. The former are natural vices; the following are supernatural virtues:

Kindness—An unselfish concern for the welfare of others, and a desire to be helpful even at great personal sacrifice.

Tenderheartedness—A sympathetic, affectionate and compassionate interest in others, and a willingness to bear their burden.

Forgiveness—A readiness to pardon offenses, to overlook personal wrongs against oneself, and to harbor no desire for retaliation.

The greatest example of One who forgives is God Himself. The basis of His forgiveness is the work of Christ at Calvary. And we are the unworthy objects.

The Authorized Version says, "even as God for Christ's sake hath forgiven you." This might give the impression that God was somewhat reluctant to forgive, but that Christ pled with Him to do it, and so for the sake of Christ He did. But this is not true. The proper translation is: "as God in Christ forgave you." God could not forgive sin without proper satisfaction being made. In His love He provided the satisfaction which His righteousness demanded. In Christ, that is, in His person and work, God found a righteous basis on which He could forgive us.

Since He forgave us when we were in debt "millions of dollars," we ought to forgive others when they owe us "a few dollars" (Matt. 18:23-35. JBP). "The moment a man wrongs me I must forgive him. Then *my* soul is free. If I hold the wrong against him, I sin against God, and against him, and jeopardize my forgiveness with God. Whether the man repents, makes amends, asks my pardon or not, makes no difference. I have instantly forgiven him. He must face God with the wrong he has done; but that is his affair and God's and not mine, save that I should help him according to Matthew 18:15, etc. But whether this succeeds or not and before this even begins, I must forgive him" (Lenski).

5

IX Exhortations to a Worthy Walk (continued) (4:1–6:9)

C. Appeal for a New Morality (continued) (4:17–5:21)

7. Hot heads and tender hearts (continued) (4:31-5:2)

c. A divine Person to imitate (5:1): *Therefore be imitators of God, as beloved children* (RSV)

d. A walk of love to duplicate (5:2): *And walk in love*

1) The perfect Model: *as Christ also*
2) The amazing fact: *hath loved us*
3) The proof: *and hath given himself for us*
4) The nature of His gift: *an offering and a sacrifice to God*
5) Its value to God: *for a sweetsmelling savour*

5:1 God's example of forgiveness in 4:32 forms the basis of Paul's exhortation here. The connection is this: God in Christ has forgiven you. Now be imitators of God in forgiving one another.

A special motive is appended in the words "as beloved children." In natural life, children bear the family likeness and should seek to uphold the family name. In spiritual life, we should manifest our Father to the world and seek to walk worthy of our dignity as His beloved children.

5:2 Another way in which we should resemble the Lord is by walking in love. The rest of the verse explains that to walk in love means to give ourselves for others. This is what

Christ, our perfect example did. Amazing fact! He loved us. The proof of His love is that He gave Himself for us in death at Calvary.

His gift is described as an offering and a sacrifice to God. An offering is anything given to God; a sacrifice here includes the additional element of death. He was the true burnt offering, the One who was completely devoted to do the will of God, even to the death of the cross. His act of unspeakable devotion is eulogized as "an offering and a sacrifice to God *for a sweetsmelling savour.*" "In love so measureless, so reckless of cost, for those who were naturally so unworthy of it, there was a spectacle which filled heaven with fragrance and God's heart with joy" (F. B. Meyer).

The Lord Jesus pleased His Father by giving Himself for others. The moral is that we too can bring joy to God by giving ourselves for others.

> Others, Lord, yes, others!
> Let this my motto be.
> Help me to live for others
> That I may live like Thee.

8. Sexual sins and saintly separation (5:3-14)
   a. Forms of sexual immorality (v. 3): *But fornication, and all uncleanness, or covetousness*
      1) The command: *let it not be once named among you*
      2) The reason: *as becometh saints*

   b. Forms of suggestive speech (v. 4): *Neither filthiness, nor foolish talking, nor jesting*
      1) An accurate appraisal: *which are not fitting* (RSV)
      2) A suitable substitute: *but rather giving of thanks*

   c. God's verdict on immoral persons (vv. 5-6)
      1) No room for doubt (v. 5): *For this ye know*
      2) No vile offenders (v. 5): *that no whoremonger, nor unclean person, nor covetous man, who is an idolater*

3) No admittance (v. 5): *hath any inheritance in the kingdom of Christ and of God*

4) No deception (v. 6): *Let no man deceive you with vain words*

5) No mercy (v. 6): *for because of these things cometh the wrath of God upon the sons of disobedience* (RV)

d. The Christian's Responsibility (vv. 7-14)

1) Positive policy (v. 7): *Be not ye therefore partakers with them*

2) Past position (v. 8): *For once you were darkness* (RSV)

3) Present position (v. 8): *but now are ye light in the Lord*

4) Proper practice (vv. 8-14)

a) Walk (vv. 8-10): *walk as children of light*
   i. Producing (v. 9): *for the fruit of light is found in all that is good and right and true* (RSV)
   ii. Proving (v. 10): *Proving what is acceptable unto the Lord*

b) Abstain (v. 11): *And have no fellowship with the unfruitful works of darkness*

c) Expose (vv. 11-14): *but instead expose them* (RSV)
   i. Their shameful character (v. 12): *For it is a shame even to speak of those things which are done of them in secret*
   ii. Their exposure by reproof (v. 13): *But all things that are reproved are made manifest by the light*
   iii. Their transformation by exposure (v. 13): *for everything that is made manifest is light* (RV)
   iv. A summons to awake and arise (v. 14: *Wherefore he saith, Awake thou that sleepest, and arise from the dead*
   v. An assurance of illumination (v. 14): *and Christ shall give thee light*

5:3 In verses 3-4, the apostle reverts to the topic of sexual sins and decisively calls for saintly separation from them.

First of all, he mentions various forms of sexual immorality.

Fornication. Whenever it is mentioned in the same verse as adultery, fornication means illicit intercourse among *unmarried* persons. However, when, as here, the word is not distinguished from adultery, it probably refers to *any* form of immorality. (Our word "pornography," literally, "whore-writing," is derived from the word translated *fornication.*)

Uncleanness. This too may mean immoral acts, but perhaps it can also include impure pictures, obscene books, and other suggestive materials that go along with lives of indecency and that feed the fires of passion.

Covetousness. While we generally think of this as meaning the lust for money, here it refers to sensual desire—the insatiable greed to satisfy one's sexual appetite outside the bounds of marriage. (See Exodus 20:17: "Thou shalt not covet . . . thy neighbour's wife, . . .")

These things should not even be named among Christians. It goes without saying that they should never have to be named as *having been committed* by believers. They should not even be *discussed* in any way that might lessen their sinful and shameful character. There is always the greatest danger in speaking lightly of them, making excuses for them, or even of discussing them familiarly and continually.

The apostle accents his exhortation with the phrase "as becometh saints." Believers have been separated from the corruption that is in the world; now they should live in practical separation from dark passion, both in deed and in word.

5:4 Their speech should also be free from every trace of:

Filthiness. No doubt this refers to dirty stories, suggestive jokes with a sexual coloring, and all forms of obscenity and indecency.

Foolish talking basically means empty conversation that is worthy of a moron. Here it probably includes gutter language.

Jesting can mean coarse jokes or talk with unsavory, hidden meanings. It has been said, "To talk about a thing, to jest about a thing, to make it a frequent subject of conversation is to introduce it into the mind, and to bring nearer the actual doing of it."

It is always dangerous to joke about sin.

Instead of using his tongue for such unworthy and unbecoming talk, the Christian should deliberately cultivate the practice of expressing thanks to God for all the blessings and mercies of life. This is pleasing to the Lord, a good example to others and beneficial to one's own soul.

5:5 There is no room for doubt as to God's attitude toward immoral persons; they have no inheritance in the kingdom of Christ and of God.

This verdict is in sharp contrast to the world's current attitude that sex offenders are sick and need psychiatric treatment. Men say immorality is a sickness; God calls it sin. Men condone it; God condemns it. Men say the answer is psychoanalysis; God says the answer is regeneration.

Three classes of offenders are specified, the same three classes that were found in verse 3—whoremongers, or fornicators, unclean persons and covetous men. Here the thought is added that a covetous person is an idolator. One reason he is an idolator is that he has a false impression of what God is like; his concept of God is a Being who approves sensual greed; otherwise, he would not dare to be covetous. Another reason why covetousness is idolatry is because it puts the person's own will above the will of God. A third reason is because it results in the worship of the creature rather than the Creator (Rom. 1:25).

When Paul says that such persons have no inheritance in the kingdom, he means precisely that. People whose lives are characterized by these sins are lost, are in their sins, and are on the way to hell. They are not in the invisible kingdom at the present time; they will not be in the kingdom when Christ returns to reign; and they will be forever shut out from the everlasting kingdom in heaven.

The apostle is not saying that these are people who, though they are in the kingdom, will suffer loss at the Judgment Seat of Christ. The subject is salvation, not rewards. They may profess to be Christians, but they prove by their lives that they were never saved.

They *can* be saved, of course, by repentance and faith in the Lord Jesus. But if they are genuinely converted, they will no longer practice these sins.

Notice that the deity of Christ is implied in the expression, "the kingdom of Christ and God" (ASV). Christ is put on an equal level with God the Father as Ruler in the kingdom.

5:6 Many men of the world adopt an increasingly lenient and tolerant attitude toward sexual immorality. They say that the gratification of bodily appetites is needful and beneficial, and that their repression produces warped, inhibited personalities. They say that morals are entirely a matter of the culture in which we live, and that since fornication, adultery and perversion are accepted in our culture, they ought to be legalized. Surprisingly enough, some of the leading spokesmen in favor of making sexual sins acceptable are men who hold high positions in the professing church. Thus, the laymen who always thought that immorality was immoral are now being assured by prominent clergymen that such an attitude is passé.

Christians should not be hoodwinked by such double talk. Because of such an attitude, God's wrath comes on the sons of disobedience.

The Lord's attitude toward such sins as fornication and adultery was seen in Numbers 25:1-9; twenty-four thousand Israelites were slain because they sinned with the women of Moab.

The Lord's attitude toward homosexuality was displayed when Sodom and Gomorrah were destroyed by brimstone and fire from heaven (Gen. 19:24, 28).

But God's wrath is displayed not only in such supernatural acts of violence. Those who practice sexual sins experience His judgment in other ways. There are physical effects, such as venereal disease. There are mental, nervous and emotional disorders arising from a sense of guilt. There are changes in the personality—the effeminate often becomes more feminine (Rom. 1:27).

And of course there will be the final, eternal judgment of God on whoremongers and adulterers (Heb. 13:4). No mercy will be shown to the sons of disobedience—to those who are descended from disobedient Adam and who willfully follow him in disobeying God (Rev. 21:8).

5:7 Believers are solemnly warned to have no part in such ungodly behavior. To do so is to dishonor the name of Christ, to wreck other lives, to ruin one's own testimony and to invite a torrent of retribution.

5:8 To enforce his urgent imperative in verse 7, the apostle now gives a pithy discourse on light and darkness (vv. 8-14).

The Ephesians were once darkness, but now they are light in the Lord. Paul does not say that they were *in* the darkness, but that they themselves were the personification of darkness.

Now through union with the Lord, they have become light. He is light; they are in Him; so they are now light in the Lord.

Their state should henceforth correspond with their standing. They should walk as children of light.

5:9 Verse 9 is a parenthesis, explaining the type of fruit that is produced by those who walk in the light.

The fruit of light (RSV) consists of all forms of goodness, righteousness and truth. Goodness here is an inclusive term for all moral excellence. Righteousness means integrity in all dealings with God and men. Truth is honesty, equity and reality. Put them all together and you have the light of a Christ-filled life shining out in a scene of dismal darkness.

5:10 Those who walk in the light not only produce the type of fruit listed in the preceding verse, but also prove what is well-pleasing to the Lord. They put every thought, word and action to the test. What does the Lord think about this? How does it appear in His presence? Every area of life comes under the searchlight—conversation, standard of living, clothes, books, business, pleasures, furniture, friendships, vacations, automobiles and sports.

5:11 Believers should have no fellowship with the unfruitful works of darkness, either by participation or by any attitude that might indicate tolerance or leniency.

Notice the expression "the unfruitful works of darkness." They are unfruitful as far as God and men are concerned. It was this feature of utter barrenness that once prompted Paul to ask the Roman Christians, "What fruit had ye then in those things whereof ye are now ashamed?" (Rom. 6:21). Then too they are works of darkness; they belong to the world of dim lights, of drawn drapes, of locked doors, of secret rooms. They reflect man's natural preferences for darkness and his abhorrence of light when his deeds are evil (John 3:19).

The believer is called not only to abstain from the unfruitful works of darkness, but positively he is called to reprove and expose them. He does this in two ways: first by a life of holiness, and second by words of correction spoken under the direction of the Holy Spirit.

5:12 Now the apostle explains why the Christian must have no complicity with moral corruption and must rebuke it. The vile sins which men commit in secret are so debased that it is a shame even to mention them, let alone to commit them. The unnatural forms of sin which man has invented are so bad that even to describe them would defile the minds of those who listened. So the Christian is taught to refrain from even talking about them.

5:13 Light makes manifest whatever is in the darkness. So a holy Christian life reveals by contrast the sinfulness of unregenerate lives. And appropriate words of rebuke reveal sin in its true character also. "As for instance when our Lord reproved the hypocrisy of the Pharisees—their practices had not seemed to the disciples very evil before, but when Christ threw on them the pure light of truth, they were made manifest in their true character—they appeared and they still appear odious" (Pulpit Commentary).

The latter part of verse 13 should read: "for everything that is made manifest is light." Which simply means that when Christians exercise their ministry as light, others are brought to the light. Wicked men are transformed into children of light through the reproving ministry of light.

It is not a rule without exceptions, of course. Not everyone who is exposed to the light becomes a Christian. But it is a general principle in the spiritual realm that light has a way of reproducing itself. We find an illustration of the principle in I Peter 3:1 where believing wives are taught to win their unbelieving husbands to Christ by the example of their lives: "In the same way you women must accept the authority of your husbands, so that if there are any of them who disbelieve the Gospel, they may be won over, without a word being said, by observing the chaste and reverent behaviour of their wives" (NEB). Thus the light of Christian wives triumphs over the darkness of heathen husbands and the latter become light.

In his expanded paraphrase of verse 13, Bruce captures this thought, as follows: "And whatever abandons the darkness and is made manifest by the light belongs henceforth to the light."

5:14 Thus the life of the believer should always be preaching a sermon, should always be exposing the surrounding darkness, should always be extending this invitation to unbelievers: "Awake, thou that sleepest, and arise from the dead, and Christ shall shine upon thee" (RV).

This is the voice of light speaking to those who are sleeping in darkness and lying in spiritual death. The light calls them to life and to illumination. If they answer the invitation, Christ will shine upon them and give them light.

9. Foolish footsteps and careful conduct (vv. 15-21):
   See then that ye walk circumspectly
   a. Negative (v. 15): *not as fools*
   b. Positive (vv. 15-16): *but as wise*
      1) Opportunity (v. 16): *redeeming the time*
      2) Urgency (v. 16): *because the days are evil*
   c. Negative (v. 17): *Wherefore be yet not unwise*
   d. Positive (v. 17): *but understanding what the will of the Lord is*
   e. Negative (v. 18a): *And be not drunk with wine, wherein is excess*
   f. Positive (v. 18b-21): *but be filled with the Spirit*
      1) Speaking (v. 19): *speaking one to another in psalms and hymns and spiritual songs* (RV)
      2) Singing (v. 19): *singing and making melody to the Lord with all your heart* (RSV)
      3) Thanking (v. 20): *Giving thanks always for all things unto God and the Father in the name of our Lord Jesus Christ*
      4) Submitting (v. 21): *subjecting yourselves one to another in the fear of Christ* (RV)

5:15 In the next seven verses, the apostle contrasts foolish footsteps and careful conduct by a series of negative and positive exhortations.

The first is a general plea to his readers not to walk as fools but as wise. As mentioned previously, "walk" is one of the key words of the epistle; it is mentioned seven times to describe "the whole round of the activities of the individual life." To walk wisely is to live in the light of our position as God's children. To walk as fools means to descend from this high plane to the conduct of worldly men.

5:16 The walk of wisdom calls us to redeem the time or buy up the opportunities. Every day brings its opened doors, its vast potential. We can redeem the time by lives of holiness, by deeds of mercy, by words of help.

What lends special urgency to this matter is the evil character of the days in which we live. They remind us that God will not always strive with man, that the day of grace will soon close, the opportunities for worship, witness and service on earth will soon be forever ended.

5:17 So we should not be unwise but should understand what the will of the Lord is. This is crucial. Because of the abounding evil and the shortness of the time, we might be tempted to spend our days in frantic and feverish activity of our own choosing. But this would amount to nothing but wasted energy. The important thing is to find out God's will for us each day and to do it. This is the only way to be efficient and effective. It is all too possible to carry on Christian work according to our own ideas and in our own strength and be completely out of the will of God. The path of wisdom is to discern God's will for our individual lives, then to obey it to the hilt.

5:18 "And be not drunk with wine, wherein is excess." In our Western culture, such a command seems almost shocking and unnecessary, since total abstinence is the rule among so many Christians. But we must remember that the Bible was written for believers in all cultures, and that in many countries wine is still a fairly common beverage on the table. The Scriptures do not condemn the use of wine, but they do condemn its abuse.

The use of wine as a medicine is recommended (Prov. 31:6; I Tim. 5:23). The Lord Jesus made wine for use as a beverage at the wedding in Cana of Galilee (John 2:1-11).

But the use of wine becomes abuse under the following circumstances and is then forbidden:

1. When it leads to excess (Prov. 23:29-35).
2. When it becomes habit-forming (I Cor. 6:12*b*).
3. When it offends the weak conscience of another believer (Rom. 14:13; I Cor. 8:9).
4. When it hurts a Christian's testimony in the community and is therefore not to the glory of God (I Cor. 10:31).
5. When there is any doubt in the Christian's mind about it (Rom. 14:23).

Paul's recommended alternative to being drunk with wine

is being filled with the Spirit. This connection too may startle us at first, but when we compare and contrast the two states, we see why the apostle links them in this way.

First of all, there are certain similarities.

1. In both conditions, the person is under a power outside himself. In one case, it is the power of intoxicating liquor (sometimes called "spirits"); in the other case, it is the power of the Holy Spirit.
2. In both conditions, the person is fervent. On the day of Pentecost, the fervency produced by the Spirit was mistaken for that produced by new wine (Acts 2:13).
3. In both conditions, the person's speech and song are affected.
4. In both conditions, the person's walk is affected—his physical walk in the case of drunkenness and his moral behavior in the other instance.

But there are two ways in which the two conditions present sharp contrasts:

1. In the case of drunkenness, there is riot, excess and debauchery. The Spirit's filling never produces these.
2. In the case of drunkenness, there is loss of self-control. But the fruit of the Spirit is self-control (Gal. 5:23; RSV). A believer who is filled with the Spirit is never transported outside himself where he can no longer control his actions; the spirit of a prophet is always subject to the prophet (I Cor. 14:32).

Sometimes in the Bible, the filling with the Spirit seems to be presented as a sovereign gift of God. For instance, John the Baptist was filled with the Holy Spirit from his mother's womb (Luke 1:15). In such a case, the person receives it without any prior conditions to be met. It is not something for which he works or prays; the Lord gives it as He pleases.

Here in Ephesians 5:18, the believer is *commanded* to be filled with the Spirit. It involves action on his part. He must meet certain conditions. It is not automatic but the result of obedience.

For this reason the Spirit's filling should be distinguished from certain other of His ministries. It is not the same as:

1. The baptism by the Holy Spirit. This is the work of the Spirit which incorporates the believer in the body of Christ (I Cor. 12:13).

2. The indwelling. By this ministry the Comforter takes up His residence in the body of the Christian and empowers him for holiness, worship and service (John 14:16).

3. The anointing. The Spirit Himself is the anointing who teaches the child of God the things of the Lord (I John 2:27).

4. The earnest and the seal. We have already seen that the Holy Spirit as the earnest guarantees the inheritance for the saint, and as seal He guarantees the saint for the inheritance (Eph. 1:13-14).

These are some of the ministries of the Spirit which are realized in a person the moment he is saved. Everyone who is in Christ automatically has the baptism, the indwelling, the anointing, the earnest and the seal.

But the filling is different. It is not a once-for-all crisis experience in the life of a disciple; rather it is a continuous process. The literal translation of the command is "Be ye being filled with the Spirit." It may begin as a crisis experience, but it must continue thereafter as a moment-by-moment process. Today's filling will not do for tomorrow.

And certainly it is a state to be greatly desired. In fact, it is the ideal condition of the believer on earth. It means that the Holy Spirit is having His way relatively ungrieved in the life of the Christian, and that the believer is therefore fulfilling his role in the plan of God for that time.

How, then, can a believer be filled with the Spirit? The Apostle Paul does not tell us here in Ephesians; he merely commands us to be filled. But from other parts of the Word, we know that in order to be filled with the Spirit we must:

1. Confess and put away all known sin in our lives (I John 1:5-9). It is obvious that such a holy Person cannot work freely in a life where sin is condoned.

2. Yield ourselves utterly and completely to His control (Rom. 12:1-2). This involves the surrender of our will, our intellect, our body, our time, our talents and our treasures. Every area of life must be thrown open to His dominion.

3. Let the word of Christ dwell in us richly (Col. 3:16). This involves reading the Word, studying it and obeying it. When the word of Christ dwells in us richly, the same results follow (Col. 3:16) as follow the filling of the Spirit (Eph. 5:19).

4. Finally, we must be emptied of self (Gal. 2:20). To be filled with a new ingredient a cup must first be emptied of the old. To be filled with *Him*, we must first be emptied of *us*.

"Just as you have left the whole burden of your sin, and have rested on the finished work of Christ, so leave the whole burden of your life and service, and rest upon the present inworking of the Holy Spirit.

"Give yourself up, morning by morning, to be led by the Holy Spirit and go forth praising and at rest, leaving Him to manage you and your day. Cultivate the habit all through the day, of joyfully depending upon and obeying Him, expecting Him to guide, to enlighten, to reprove, to teach, to use, and to do in and with you what He wills. Count upon His working as a fact, altogether apart from sight or feeling. Only let us believe in and obey the Holy Spirit as the Ruler of our lives, and cease from the burden of trying to manage ourselves; then shall the fruit of the Spirit appear in us as He wills to the glory of God" (Author unknown).

Does a person know it when he is filled with the Spirit? Actually, the closer we are to the Lord, the more we are conscious of our own complete unworthiness and sinfulness (Isa. 6:1-5). In His presence, we find nothing in ourselves to be proud of (Luke 5:8). We are not aware of any spiritual superiority over others, any sense of "having arrived." The man who is filled with the Spirit is occupied with Christ and not with himself.

At the same time, he may have a realization that God is working in and through his life. He sees things happen in a supernatural way. Circumstances click miraculously. Lives are touched for God. Events move according to a divine timetable. Even forces of nature are on his side; they seem chained to the chariot wheels of the Lord. He sees all this; he realizes that God is working for him and through him; and yet he feels strangely detached from it all as far as taking any credit is concerned. In his inmost being, he realizes that it is all of the Lord.

5:19   Now the apostle gives four results of being filled with the Spirit.

First, Spirit-filled Christians speak to one another in psalms and hymns and spiritual songs. The divine infilling opens the mouth to talk about the things of the Lord, and enlarges the heart to share these things with others.

We understand psalms to mean the inspired writings of David, Asaph and others. Hymns are noninspired songs which ascribe worship and praise directly to God. Spiritual songs are any other lyrical compositions that deal with spiritual themes, even though not addressed directly to God.

A second evidence of the filling is inward joy and praise to God: "Singing and making melody in your heart to the Lord." The Spirit-filled life is a fountain, bubbling over with joy (Acts 13:52). The Revised Standard Version translates: "making melody . . . *with all your heart.*" Here the heart is not the place but the manner of praise. Zacharias is an illustration; when he was filled with the Holy Spirit, he sang with all his heart to the Lord (Luke 1:67-79).

5:20   A third result is thanksgiving: "Giving thanks always for all things in the name of our Lord Jesus Christ to God, even the Father" (RV). Where the Spirit reigns, there is gratitude to God, a deep sense of appreciation, and a spontaneous expression of it. It is not occasional, but continual. Not only for the pleasant things but for all things. Anyone can be thankful for sunshine; it takes the power of the Spirit to be thankful for the storms of life.

"The shortest, surest way to all happiness is this: *Make it a rule to thank and praise God for everything that happens to you.* For it is certain that whatever seeming calamity comes to you, if you thank and praise God for it, you turn it into a blessing. If you could work miracles, you could not do more for yourself than by this thankful spirit: for it needs not a word spoken and turns all that it touches into happiness" (Selected).

5:21 The fourth test of being Spirit-filled is "submitting yourselves one to another in the fear of God." "This is a phrase too often neglected. It names a test of spirituality which Christians too seldom apply. Many persons feel that shouts of hallelujah and exulting songs and the utterance of praise in more or less 'unknown tongues' are all proofs of being filled with the Spirit. These all may be spurious and deceitful and without meaning. Submission to our fellow Christians, modesty of demeanor, humility, and unwillingness to dispute, forbearance, gentleness—these are the unmistakable proofs of the Spirit's power. . . . Such mutual submission to their fellow Christians should be rendered 'in the fear of Christ,' that is, in reverence to Him Who is recognized as the Lord and Master of all" (Erdman).

These then are four of the results of the Spirit's filling—speaking, singing, thanking and submitting. But there are at least four others which we will mention briefly:

1. Boldness in rebuking sin (Acts 13:9-12), and in testifying for the Lord (Acts 4:8-12, 31; 13:52—14:3).
2. Power for service (Acts 1:8; 6:3, 8; 11:24).
3. Generosity, not selfishness (Acts 4:31-32).
4. Exaltation of Christ (Acts 9:17, 20) and of God (Acts 2:4, 11; 10:44, 46).

We should earnestly desire to be filled with the Spirit, but only for the glory of God, not for our own glory.

D. Appeal for Personal Piety in the Christian household
(5:22–6:9)

  1. Practical precepts for model marriages (5:22-33)

    a. A word to wives (vv. 22-24)

      1) Their duty (v. 22): *Wives, be in subjection* (RV)

      2) The sphere of subjection (v. 22): *unto your own husbands*

      3) The spirit of subjection (v. 22): *as unto the Lord*

      4) The reason for subjection (v. 23): *For the husband is the head of the wife*

      5) The prototype of the husband's authority (v. 23)

        a) Head: *even as Christ is the head of the church*

        b) Savior: *and he is the saviour of the body*

      6) The manner of the wives' subjection (v. 24): *Therefore as the church is subject unto Christ, so let the wives be to their own husbands*

      7) The extent of subjection (v. 24): *in every thing*

    b. A high standard for husbands (vv. 25-32)

      1) The command (v. 25): *Husbands, love your wives*

      2) The pattern of this love (v. 25): *even as Christ also loved the church*

      3) The program of Christ's love for the church (vv. 25-27)

        a) Past (v. 25): *and gave himself for it*

        b) Present (v. 26): *that he might sanctify it, cleansing it by the washing of water by the word* (FWG)

        c) Future (v. 27): *That he might present it to himself a glorious church, not having spot, or wrinkle, or any such thing; but that it should be holy and without blemish*

    4) The husband's responsibility (vv. 28-30): *So ought men to love their wives*

        a) The biblical view of the wives' position (v. 28): *as [being] their [i.e., the husbands'] own bodies. He that loveth his wife loveth himself*

        b) The natural instinct to care for one's own body (v. 29): *For no man ever yet hated his own flesh; but nourisheth and cherisheth it*

        c) The analogy of Christ and the church (vv. 29-30): *even as Christ also the church; because we are members of his body* (RV)

    5) The original concept of marriage (v. 31)

        a) The wife relationship supersedes the parental relationship: *For this cause shall a man leave his father and mother, and shall be joined unto his wife*

        b) Two persons become one: *and they two shall be one flesh*

    6) The wonderful parallel, hitherto unknown (v. 32): *This is a great mystery: but I speak concerning Christ and the church*

  c. The message, in a word, to husband and wife (v. 33)

    1) To the husband, the word is love: *Nevertheless let every one of you in particular so love his wife even as himself*

    2) To the wife, the word is respect: *and let the wife see that she respects her husband* (RSV)

5:22 Though a new section seems to begin here, there is a close link with the preceding verse. There Paul had listed subjection to one another as one of the results of the divine infilling. In the section from 5:22 to 6:9, he cites three specific areas in the Christian household where submission is the will of God:

    Wives should be subject to their husbands.
    Children should be subject to their parents.
    Servants should be subject to their masters.

The fact that all believers are one in Christ Jesus does not mean that earthly relationships are abolished. We must still respect the various forms of authority and government which God has instituted.

Every well-ordered society rests on two supporting pillars —authority and subjection. There must be some who exercise authority and some who submit to that rule. This principle is so basic that it is found even in the Godhead: "But I would have you know, that . . . the head of Christ is God" (I Cor. 11:3).

God ordained human government. No matter how wicked a government may be, yet from God's standpoint it is better than no government, and we should obey it as far as we can without disobeying or denying the Lord. The absence of government is anarchy, and no society can survive under anarchy.

The same is true in the home. There must be a head, and there must be obedience to that head. God ordained that the place of headship be given to the man. He indicated this by creating man first, then creating woman for the man. Thus, both in the order and purpose of creation, He put man in the place of authority and woman in the place of subjection.

Subjection never implies inferiority. The Lord Jesus is subject to God the Father, but in no way is He inferior to Him. Neither is the woman inferior to the man. In many ways she may be superior—in devotedness, in sympathy, in diligence, and in heroic endurance.

But she is commanded to be subject to her own husband, as unto the Lord. In submitting to the authority of her husband, she is submitting to the Lord's authority. This in itself should remove any attitude of reluctance or rebellion.

History abounds with illustrations of the chaos resulting from disobedience to God's pattern. By usurping the place of leadership, and acting for her husband, Eve introduced sin into the human race, with all its catastrophic results. In more recent times, many of the false cults were started by women who usurped a place of authority which God never intended them to have. Women who leave their God-appointed sphere can wreck a local church, can break up a marriage, and can destroy a home.

On the other hand, there is nothing more attractive than to see a woman fulfilling the role which God has assigned to her. A full-length portrait of such a woman is given in Proverbs 31—an enduring memorial to the wife and mother who pleases the Lord.

5:23 The reason given for the wife's subjection is that her husband is her head. He occupies the same relation to her that Christ occupies to the church. Christ is the Head of the church, and He is the Savior of the body. (The word Savior here can have the meaning of Preserver, as it has in I Tim. 4:10, JND). So the husband is the head of the wife, and he is her preserver as well. As head, he loves, leads and guides; as preserver, he provides, protects and cares for her.

We all know that there is a great revulsion against this teaching in our day. People accuse Paul of being a bigoted bachelor and a woman-hater. Or they say that his views reflect the social customs of that day but are no longer applicable today. Such statements are, of course, a frontal attack on the inspiration of the Scriptures. These are not Paul's words; they are the words of God. To refuse them is to refuse Him and to invite difficulty and disaster.

5:24 Nothing could more exalt the role of the wife than comparing it to the role of the church as the bride of Christ. The church's subjection is the pattern to be followed by the wife.

She is to be subject in everything—that is, everything that is in accordance with the will of God. No wife would be expected to obey her husband if he required her to compromise her loyalty to the Lord Jesus. But in all the normal relationships of life, she is to obey her husband, even if he is an unbeliever.

5:25 If the foregoing instructions to wives stood alone, if there were no correspondingly high instructions to husbands, then the presentation would be one-sided, if not unfair.

But notice the beautiful balance of truth in the Scriptures, and the corresponding standard which they require of the husbands.

Husbands are not told to keep their wives in subjection; they are told to love their wives as Christ loved the church. It has been well said that no wife would mind being subject to a husband who loves her as Christ loves the church.

Someone wrote of a man who feared he was displeasing God by loving his wife too much. A Christian worker asked him if he loved her more than Christ loved the church. He said no. "Only when you go beyond that," said the worker, "are you loving your wife too much."

Christ's love for the church is presented here in three majestic movements extending from the past to the present to the future.

In the past, He demonstrated His love for the church by giving Himself for it. This refers to His sacrificial death on the cross. There He paid the greatest price in order to purchase a bride for Himself. Just as Eve was brought forth from the side of Adam, so, in a sense, the church was created from the riven side of the Savior.

5:26   His love for the church at the present time is manifested in His work of sanctification: "that he might sanctify it, cleansing it by the washing of water by the word" (FWG).

To sanctify means to set apart. Positionally the church is already sanctified; practically it is being set apart day by day. It is going through a process of moral and spiritual preparation, similar to the one-year course of beauty culture which Esther took before being presented to King Ahasuerus (Esther 2:12-16).

The process of sanctification is carried on by the washing of water by the Word. In simple terms this means that the lives of believers are cleansed as they hear the words of Christ and obey them. Thus Jesus said to the disciples, "Already ye are clean because of the word which I have spoken unto you" (John 15:3, RV). And He linked sanctification with the Word in His high priestly prayer, "Sanctify them through thy truth: thy word is truth" (John 17:17).

Just as the blood of Christ cleanses once for all from the guilt and penalty of sin, so the Word of God cleanses continually from the defilement and pollution of sin. This passage teaches that the church is being bathed at the present time, not with literal water, but with the cleansing agent of the Word of God.

5:27 In the past, Christ's love was manifested in our redemption. In the present, it is seen in our sanctification. In the future, it will be displayed in our glorification. He Himself will present to Himself a glorious church, not having spot or wrinkle or any such thing, but holy and without blemish. It will then reach the acme of beauty and spiritual perfection.

"Think of it—when the omniscient eye looks upon us at the last, He will not find anything that to His immaculate holiness can be so much as a pimple or a mole on a human face. How incredible!" (A. T. Pierson).

"No sign of old age, no defect, nothing will suit Him then but the bloom and eternity of an eternal youth, the freshness of affections which will never tire, which can know no decay. The Church will be holy and blameless then. After all that we have known of her history, it would be strange to read this, if we did not know how gloriously God maintains His triumph over sin and evil" (FWG).

5:28 After soaring off on this magnificent rhapsody dealing with Christ's love for the church, Paul now returns to remind husbands that this is the pattern they are to imitate: "Even so ought husbands also to love their own wives as their own bodies" (RV). In imitation of Christ's love, they should love their wives as being indeed their own bodies.

In the Greek, the word "own" occurs six times in verses 22-33.

"Wives, be in subjection unto your *own* husbands" (v. 22, RV).

"So ought husbands also to love their *own* wives as their *own* bodies" (v. 28a, RV).

"He that loveth his *own* wife loveth himself" (v. 28*b*, RV).
"For no man ever hated his *own* flesh, . . ." (v. 29, RV).
"Nevertheless do ye also severally love each one his *own*
wife even as himself" (v. 33, RV).

This emphatic use of the word "own" reminds us that
monogamy is God's will for His people. Although He permitted polygamy in the Old Testament, He never approved
it.

It is also interesting to notice the varied ways in which
Paul describes the close relationship of the husband and the
wife. He says that in loving his wife, a man is loving:

> his own body (v. 28*a*)
> himself (vv. 28*b*, 33)
> his own flesh (v. 29)

Since marriage involves a true union of persons, and two
become one flesh, a man who loves his wife is, in a very real
sense, loving himself.

5:29   Man is born with the instinct to care for his own
body. He feeds it, clothes it, bathes it. And he protects it
from discomforts, pain and harm. Its continued survival de-
pends on this care. This solicitous interest is a pale shadow
of Christ's care for the church.

5:30   "For we are members of his body" (RV). The grace
of God is amazing! It not only saves us from sin and hell,
but incorporates us into Christ as members of His mystical
body. What volumes this speaks concerning His love for us;
He cherishes us as His own body. What care: He nourishes,
sanctifies and trains us. What security: He will not be in
heaven without His members.

We are united to Him in a common life. Whatever affects
the members affects the Head also.

5:31   The apostle now quotes Genesis 2:24 as presenting
God's original concept in instituting the marriage relationship.

First, the man's relationship to his parents is superseded
by a higher loyalty, that is, his loyalty to his wife. In order

to realize the high ideal of the marital relationship, he leaves his parents and cleaves to his wife.

The second feature is that husband and wife become one flesh; there is a real union of two persons.

If these two basic facts were kept in mind, they would eliminate in-law troubles on the one hand, and marital strife on the other.

5:32 "This mystery is great: but I speak in regard of Christ and of the church" (RV). Paul now climaxes his discussion of the marriage relationship by announcing this wonderful truth, hitherto unknown, namely, that as a wife is to her husband, so the church is to Christ.

When Paul says that the mystery is great, he does not mean that it is very mysterious. Rather he means that the implications of the truth are tremendous. The mystery is the wonderful purpose which was hidden in God in previous ages, but which has now been revealed. That purpose is to call out of the nations a people to become the body and bride of His glorious Son. The human marriage relationship thus finds its perfect antitype in the relation between Christ and the church.

> One spirit with the Lord
> Jesus, the glorified
> Esteems the church for which He bled
> His body and His bride

5:33 This final verse is a sentence summary of what the apostle has been saying to husbands and wives.

To the husbands, the concluding admonition is this: let every one of you, without exception, love his wife as being himself. Not merely as you might love yourself, but in recognition of the fact that she is one with you.

To the wives the word is: see that you continually respect and obey your husbands.

Now stop and think for a moment! What would happen if these divine instructions were followed by Christian people today? The answer is obvious. There would be no strife, no separation, no divorce. Our homes would be more like foretastes of heaven than they often are.

6

IX. Exhortations to a Worthy Walk (continued) (4:1–6:9)

D. Appeal for Personal Piety in the Christian Household (continued) (5:22–6:9)

  2. Obedient children and pattern parents (6:1-4)
    a. What God has to say to children (vv. 1-3)
      1) Their basic duty (v. 1): *Children, obey your parents*
      2) The nature and extent of their obedience (v. 1) *in the Lord*
      3) The reasons why they should obey (vv. 1-3)
        a) It is right (v. 1): *for this is right*
        b) It is scriptural (v. 2): *Honour thy father and mother; which is the first commandment with promise*
        c) It is for their own best interests (v. 3): *That it may be well with thee*
        d) It promotes a full life (v. 3): *and thou mayest live long on the earth*
    b. What God has to say to fathers (v. 4)
      1) Negative: *And, ye fathers, provoke not your children to wrath*
      2) Positive: *but bring them up in the nurture and admonition of the Lord*

6:1 In the previous chapters we learned that one of the results of being filled with the Spirit is being submissive to one another. We saw that a Spirit-filled wife, for instance, is subject to her husband. Now we learn that Spirit-filled children willingly submit to the authority of their parents.

The fundamental duty of all children is to obey their parents in the Lord. Whether the children are Christians or whether the parents are Christians does not make any difference. The parent-child relationship was ordained for all mankind, not just for believers.

The command to "obey . . . in the Lord" means, first of all, that children should obey with the attitude that in doing so they are obeying the Lord; their obedience should be as unto Him. Second, it means that they should obey in all matters which are in accordance with the will of God. If their parents ordered them to sin, they should not be expected to comply. In such a case they should courteously refuse and suffer the consequences meekly and without retaliation. However, in all other cases they must be obedient.

Four reasons are given why they should obey. First of all, it is right. It is a basic principle built into the very structure of family life that those who are immature, impulsive and inexperienced should submit to the authority of parents who are older and wiser.

6:2 The second reason is that it is scriptural. Here Paul quotes Exodus 20:12: "Honour thy father and thy mother" (see also Deut. 5:16). This command to honor parents is the first of the Ten Commandments with a specific promise of blessing attached to it. It calls for children to respect, love and obey their parents.

6:3 The third reason is that it is for the best interests of the children: "that it may be well with thee." Think of what would happen to a child who received no instruction and no correction from his parents! He would be personally miserable and socially intolerable.

The fourth reason is that obedience promotes a full life: "and thou mayest live long on the earth." In the Old Testament, a Jewish child who obeyed his parents actually did enjoy a long life. In this gospel age, it is not a rule without exceptions. Filial obedience is not always connected with longevity. A dutiful son may die at an early age. But it is true in a general way that the life of discipline and obedience is conducive to health and longevity, whereas a life of rebellion and recklessness often ends prematurely.

6:4 The instructions to children are now balanced with advice to fathers. They should not provoke their children to anger with unreasonable demands, with undue harshness, with constant nagging.

Rather children should be nurtured in the chastening and admonition of the Lord. Chastening means discipline and correction and may be verbal or corporal. Admonition means warning, rebuke, reproof. Child-training should be "in the Lord," that is, carried out in accordance with His will as revealed in the Bible by one who acts as His representative.

Susannah Wesley, the mother of seventeen children, including John and Charles, once wrote: "The parent who studies to subdue self-will in his child, works together with God in the renewing and saving of a soul. The parent who indulges it, does the Devil's work, makes religion impractical, salvation unattainable, and does all that in him lies to damn his child, soul and body forever."

    3. Sincere servants and noble masters (6:5-9)

        a. What is expected of Christian servants (vv. 5-8)

            1) They should obey (v. 5): *Servants, be obedient to them that are your masters according to the flesh*

            2) They should be respectful (v. 5): *with fear and trembling*

            3) They should be conscientious (v. 5): *in singleness of your heart*

            4) They should serve for Christ (v. 5): *as unto Christ*

            5) They should always be diligent (v. 6)

                a) Not only when their employer is looking (v. 6): *Not with eyeservice, as menpleasers*

                b) But conscious that the Master is always looking (v. 6): *but as the servants of Christ*

                c) And anxious to please God (v. 6): *doing the will of God from the heart*

            6) They should serve cheerfully (v. 7): *With good will doing service*

            7) They should view all service as sacred (v. 7): *as to the Lord, and not to men*

        8) They should be assured that they will be re-
warded (v. 8)

          a) The basis of reward: *Knowing that what-
soever good thing any man doeth*

          b) The promise of reward: *the same shall he
receive*

          c) The source of reward: *of the Lord*

          d) Eligibility for reward: *whether he be
bond or free*

     b. What is expected of Christian masters (v. 9)

        1) Kind treatment: *And, ye masters, do the same
things unto them*

        2) No threats: *forbearing threatening*

        3) Realization that they too are servants: *know-
ing that he who is both their Master and yours
is in heaven* (ASV)

        4) Remembrance that their Master is impartial:
neither is there respect of persons with him

6:5 The third and final sphere of submission in the Christian household is that of servants to masters. The word Paul
uses is "bondslaves," but the principles apply to servants or
employees of all types.

The first duty of employees is to obey those who are their
masters according to the flesh. The expression "masters according to the flesh" reminds us that the employer has juris-
diction as far as physical or mental work are concerned, but
he cannot dictate in spiritual matters or command the conscience.

Second, servants should be respectful. Fear and trembling
do not mean cowering servility and abject terror; they mean
a dutiful respect and a fear of offending the Lord and the
employer.

Third, service should be conscientious, or "in singleness of
heart." We should endeavor to deliver sixty minutes of work
for every hour of pay.

Next, our work should be "as unto Christ." These words
show that there need be no real distinction between the
secular and the sacred. All that we do should be for Him—

with a view to pleasing Him, to honoring Him and to attracting others to Him. The most menial and commonplace tasks in life are ennobled and dignified when they are done for the glory of God. Even dishwashing! That is why some Christian housewives have this motto over their kitchen sink: "Divine service held here three times daily."

6:6 We should always be diligent, not only when the boss is looking, but conscious that our Master is always looking. It is a natural tendency to slack off when the employer is away, but it is a form of dishonesty. The Christian's standards of performance should not vary according to the geographical location of the foreman.

A customer once urged a Christian sales clerk to give him more than he was paying for, assuring him that his employer was not looking. The sales clerk replied, "My Master is always looking!"

As servants of Christ, we should do the will of God from the heart, that is, with a sincere desire to please Him. "Labor is unmeasurably dignified by such considerations as these. The task of the humblest slave may be ennobled by being rendered in such a way as to please Christ, with such good will, with such hearty readiness and zeal, as to merit the approval of the Lord" (Erdman).

6:7 Then, too, we should serve with good will. Not with an outward display of compliance while we are inwardly seething with resentment, but cheerfully and willingly.

Even if a master is overbearing, abusive and unreasonable, our work can still be done as to the Lord and not to men. It is this type of supernatural behavior that speaks the loudest in the kind of world in which we live.

6:8 A great incentive to do all as unto Christ is the assurance that He will reward every such good work. Whether a person is a slave or a free man makes no difference. The Lord notes all the jobs, pleasant or disagreeable, that are done for Him and He will reward each worker.

Before leaving this section on slaves, some comments should be made:

1. The New Testament does not condemn slavery as such. In fact, it likens the true believer to a slave of Christ (v. 6, NEB). But the abuses of slavery have disappeared wherever the gospel has gone—not by forcible revolution but by moral reformation.

2. The New Testament has more to say to slaves than it has to kings. This may be a reflection of the fact that not many wise, mighty or noble are called (I Cor. 1:26). Probably most Christians are found in the lower economic and social brackets. The emphasis on slaves also shows that the most menial servants are not excluded from the choicest blessings of Christianity.

3. The effectiveness of these instructions to slaves is seen in the fact that in the early days of Christianity, Christian slaves almost invariably brought higher prices at the auction than heathen bondservants. It should be true today that Christian employees are worth more to their employers than those who have never been touched by the grace of God.

6:9 Masters should be guided by the same general principles as servants. They should be fair, kind and honest.

They should be particularly careful to refrain from abusive and threatening language. If they exercise discipline in this area, they will never have to resort to physical abuse of their servants.

And they should always remember that they too have a Master, the same Master in heaven that the slave has. Earthly distinctions are leveled in the presence of the Lord. Both master and servant will one day give an account to Him.

X. Exhortations Concerning the Christian Warfare (6:10-20)

    A. The Need for Divine Power (v. 10): *Finally, be strong in the Lord and in the strength of his might* (RSV)

    B. The Need for Divine Armor (vv. 11-13): *Put on the whole armour of God*

     1. In order to stand (v. 11): *that ye may be able to stand against the wiles of the devil*

     2. In order to wrestle (v. 12): *For we wrestle*
        a. Not against men: *not against flesh and blood*
        b. Against evil spirits: *but against the principalities, against the powers, against the world-rulers of this darkness, against the spiritual hosts of wickedness in the heavenly places* (RV)

     3. In order to withstand (v. 13): *Wherefore take unto you the whole armour of God, that ye may be able to withstand in the evil day*

     4. In order to stand (v. 13): *and having done all, to stand*

C. The Need to Stand, Equipped with the Armor (vv. 14-17): *Stand therefore*

     1. The belt (v. 14): *having your loins girt about with truth*

     2. The breastplate (v. 14): *and having on the breastplate of righteousness*

     3. The sandals (v. 15): *And your feet shod with the preparation of the gospel of peace*

     4. The shield (v. 16): *Above all, taking the shield of faith, wherewith ye shall be able to quench all the fiery darts of the wicked*

     5. The helmet (v. 17): *And take the helmet of salvation*

     6. The sword (v. 17): *and the sword of the Spirit, which is the word of God*

D. The Need for Prayer (vv. 18-20)

     1. At all times (v. 18): *Praying always*

     2. All kinds of prayer (v. 18): *with all prayer and supplication*

     3. Spirit-led prayer (v. 18): *in the Spirit*

     4. Vigilance in prayer (v. 18): *and watching thereunto*

     5. Perseverance in prayer (v. 18): *with all perseverance*

     6. Prayer for all saints (v. 18): *and supplication for all saints*

     7. Paul's need for prayer (vv. 19-20): *And for me*
        a. For fluency (v. 19): *that utterance may be given unto me*

       b. For boldness (vv. 19-20): *that I may open my mouth boldly*
          1) The message (v. 19): *to make known the mystery of the gospel*
          2) The messenger (v. 20): *For which I am an ambassador in bonds*
       c. For courageous obedience (v. 20): *that therein I may speak boldly, as I ought to speak*

6:10 Now the Apostle Paul is coming to the close of his epistle. Addressing all the family of God, he makes a stirring appeal to them as soldiers of Christ.

Every true child of God soon learns that the Christian life is a warfare. The hosts of Satan are committed to hinder and obstruct the work of Christ and to knock the individual soldier out of combat. The more effective a believer is for the Lord, the more he will experience the savage attacks of the enemy; the devil does not waste his ammunition on nominal Christians.

In our own strength we are no match for the devil. So the first preparatory command is that we should be continually strengthened in the Lord and in the boundless resources of His might. God's best soldiers are those who are conscious of their own weakness and ineffectiveness, and who rely solely on Him. "God hath chosen the weak things of the world to confound the things which are mighty" (I Cor. 1:27*b*). Our weakness commends itself to the strength of His might.

6:11 The second command is concerned with the need for divine armor. The believer must put on the whole armor of God that he may be able to stand against the stratagems of the devil. It is necessary to be completely armed; one or two pieces will not do. Nothing less than the whole panoply which God provides will keep us invulnerable.

The devil has various stratagems—discouragement, frustration, confusion, moral failure and doctrinal error. He knows our weakest point and aims for it. If he cannot disable us by one method, he will try another.

6:12 This warfare is not a matter of contending against godless philosophers, crafty priests, Christ-denying cultists or infidel rulers. The battle is against demonic forces, against battalions of fallen angels, against evil spirits who wield tremendous power.

Though we cannot see them, we are constantly surrounded by wicked spirit-beings. While it is true that they cannot indwell a true believer, they can oppress and harass him. The Christian need not be morbidly occupied with the subject of demonism; neither need he live in fear of demons. In the armor of God, he has all that he needs to hold his ground against their onslaughts.

The apostle speaks of these fallen angels as principalities; powers; rulers of the darkness of this world, (literally, cosmocrats of this darkness); and spiritual wickedness in high places, (literally, evil spirit-beings in the heavenlies). We do not have sufficient knowledge to distinguish between these; perhaps they refer to spirit-rulers with differing degrees of authority, such as presidents, governors, mayors and aldermen, on the human scale.

6:13 As Paul wrote, he was probably guarded by a Roman soldier in full armor. Always quick to see spiritual lessons in the natural realm, he makes the application: we are flanked by formidable foes; we must put on the whole armor of God that we might be able to stand when the conflict reaches its fiercest intensity, and still be found standing when the smoke of battle has cleared away.

"The evil day" probably refers to any time when the enemy comes against us like a flood. Satanic opposition seems to occur in waves, advancing and receding. Even after our Lord's temptation in the wilderness, the devil left Him for a season (Luke 4:13).

6:14 The first piece of armor mentioned is the girdle or belt of truth. Certainly we must be faithful in holding the truth of God's Word, but it is also necessary for the truth to hold us. We must apply it to our daily lives. As we test everything by the truth, we find strength and protection in the combat.

The second piece is the breastplate of righteousness. Every believer is clothed with the righteousness of God (II Cor. 5:21), but he must also manifest integrity and uprightness in his personal life. Someone has said, "When a man is clothed in practical righteousness, he is impregnable. Words are no defense against accusation, but a good life is." If our conscience is void of offense toward God and man, the devil has nothing to shoot at. David put on the breastplate of righteousness in Psalm 7:3-5. The Lord Jesus wore it at all times (Isa. 59:17).

6:15 The soldier's feet must be "shod with the preparation of the gospel of peace." This suggests a readiness to go forth with the good news of peace, and therefore an invasion into enemy territory. When we relax in our tents, we are in deadly peril. Our safety is to be found in following the beautiful feet of the Savior on the mountains, bearing good tidings and publishing peace (Isa. 52:7; Rom. 10:15).

> Take my feet and let them be
> Swift and beautiful for Thee

6:16 In addition, the soldier must take the shield of faith so that when the fiery darts of the evil one come zooming at him, they will hit the shield and fall harmlessly to the ground. Faith here is firm confidence in the Lord and in His Word. When temptations burn, when circumstances are adverse, when doubts assail, when shipwreck threatens, faith looks up and says, "I believe God."

6:17 The helmet God provides is salvation (Isa. 59:17). No matter how hot the battle, the Christian is not daunted since he knows that ultimate victory is sure. Assurance of eventual deliverance preserves him from retreat or surrender. "If God be for us, who can be against us?" (Rom. 8:31).

Finally, the soldier takes the Sword of the Spirit which is the Word of God. The classic illustration of this, of course, is our Lord's use of this sword in His encounter with Satan. Three times He quoted the Word of God—not just random

verses but the appropriate verses which the Holy Spirit gave
Him for that occasion (Luke 4:1-13).

When Paul speaks of the Word of God here, he does not
mean the whole Bible as such, but the particular portion of
the Bible which best suits the occasion.

6:18   Prayer is not mentioned as a part of the armor; but
we would not be overrating its importance if we say that it
is the atmosphere in which the soldier must live and breathe.
It is the spirit in which he must don the armor and face the
foe.

Prayer should be continual, not sporadic; a habit, not an
isolated act.

Then too the soldier should use all kinds of prayer: public
and private; deliberate and spontaneous; supplication and
intercession; confession and humiliation; praise and thanksgiving.

And prayer should be in the Spirit, that is, inspired and led
by Him. Formal, ritualistic, liturgical prayers—of what value
are they in combat against the hosts of hell?

There must be vigilance in prayer: "watching thereunto."
We must watch against drowsiness, against mind-wandering,
against preoccupation with other things. Prayer requires
spiritual keenness, alertness and concentration.

And there must be perseverance in prayer. We must keep
on asking, seeking, knocking (Luke 11:9).

Supplication should be made for all saints. They are engaged in the conflict too, and need to be supported in prayer
by their fellow soldiers.

6:19   " 'And for me.' Mark the unpriestly idea. So far
from Paul having a store of grace for all the Ephesians, he
needed their prayers, that out of the one living store, the
needful grace might be given to him" (Pulpit Commentary).

The apostle was writing from prison. Yet he did not ask
prayer for his early release. Rather he asked for utterance
in opening his mouth to declare the mystery of the gospel.
He wanted the message to go out with all boldness.

This is Paul's final mention of the mystery in this epistle. Here it is presented as the reason for his bonds. Yet he has no regrets. On the contrary, he wants to broadcast it more and more.

6:20 Ambassadors are generally granted diplomatic immunity from arrest and imprisonment. But men will tolerate almost anything better than they will tolerate the gospel. No other subject stirs such emotion, arouses such hostility and suspicion, and provokes such persecution. So Christ's representative was an ambassador in chains. "A legate from the mightiest Sovereignty, charged with an embassy of unparalleled nobleness and urgency, and bearing with him credentials of unmistakable authenticity, is detained in captivity" (Eadie).

The particular part of Paul's message that stirred the hostility of narrow religionists was the announcement that believing Jews and believing Gentiles are now formed into one new society, sharing equal privileges, and acknowledging Christ as Head.

XI. Personal Greetings from the Apostle (6:21-24)

    A. News for the Saints (vv. 21-22)

        1. Subject (v. 21): *But that ye also may know my affairs, and how I do*

        2. Reporter (v. 21): *Tychicus, a beloved brother and faithful minister in the Lord*

        3. Coverage (v. 21): *shall make known to you all things*

        4. Twofold object (v. 22): *Whom I have sent unto you for this very purpose* (RV)

          a. Information: *that ye might know our affairs*

          b. Encouragement: *and that he may encourage your hearts* (RSV)

    B. Peace and Love to the Saints (v. 23): *Peace be to the brethren, and love with faith, from God the Father and the Lord Jesus Christ*

    C. Grace to the Saints (v. 24): *Grace with all them that love our Lord Jesus Christ in incorruption* (JND)

6:21 In verses 21-24, the epistle is closed with personal greetings. Paul was sending Tychicus from Rome to Ephesus to let the saints know how he was getting along. He commends Tychicus as a beloved brother and a faithful servant in the Lord.

There are only five references to this man in the New Testament. He was one of the party that traveled with Paul from Greece to Asia (Acts 20:4). He was the apostle's messenger to the Christians at Colosse (Col. 4:7); to Ephesus (cf. 6:21 with II Tim. 4:12) and possibly to Titus in Crete (Titus 3:12). (His name is pronounced Tick-icus, with the accent on the first syllable.)

6:22 His twofold mission at this time was to inform the saints concerning Paul's welfare in prison, and also to encourage their hearts, allaying any unnecessary fears.

6:23 In the closing verses, we have Paul's characteristic greetings—peace and grace. In combining these two, he wishes for his readers the sum of all blessings. Also in combining the characteristic Jewish and Gentile greetings, he may be making a final veiled reference to the mystery of the gospel—Jew and Gentile now made one in Christ.

In verse 23, he desires that his readers may have peace and love with faith. Peace would garrison their hearts in every circumstance of life. Love would enable them to worship God and work with one another. Faith would empower them for exploits in the Christian warfare.

All these blessings come from God the Father and the Lord Jesus Christ, a fact that would be impossible if They were not equal.

6:24 Finally the beloved apostle wishes grace for all who love the Lord Jesus Christ with an incorruptible love. True Christian love has the quality of permanence; its flame may flicker and grow low at times but it is never extinguished.

CONCLUSION

The Roman prison has long since given up its noble inmate. The great apostle has entered into his reward and seen the face of his Beloved. But the letter is still with us—as fresh and alive as the day it came from his heart and pen. In the twentieth century it still speaks to us words of instruction, inspiration, conviction and exhortation.

"There is perhaps no writing in the Book of God so majestic and so wonderful: and therefore, how impossible it is for any man, as a messenger even from God Himself, to do justice to it in the space allotted to us! I hope we may draw nigh to it, simply seeking for teachings upon holiness, teachings by which we may be sent forth to live a nobler and higher life than hitherto, and by which we may be enabled to glorify God" (H. W. Webb-Peploe).

BIBLIOGRAPHY

BELLETT, J. G. *Brief Notes on the Epistle to the Ephesians.* London: G. Morrish, n.d.

BLAIKIE, W. G. "Ephesians," *Pulpit Commentary.* Vol. 20. Grand Rapids: Wm. B. Eerdmans Publishing Co., 1950.

BRUCE, F. F. *The Letters of Paul, An Expanded Paraphrase.* Grand Rapids: Wm. B. Eerdmans Publishing Co., 1965.

CHAFER, L. S. *Systematic Theology.* Dallas: Dallas Seminary Press, 1947.

DALE, R. W. *The Epistle to the Ephesians; Its Doctrine and Ethics,* quoted in Eadie's commentary (see below).

EADIE, JOHN. *Commentary on the Epistle to the Ephesians.* Grand Rapids: Zondervan Publishing House, 1957.

ERDMAN, CHARLES R. *The Epistle of Paul to the Ephesians.* Philadelphia: Westminster Press, 1931.

HAVNER, VANCE. *Why Not Just Be Christians?* New York: Fleming H. Revell Co., 1964.

JAMIESON, FAUSSET and BROWN. *Commentary Practical and Explanatory on the Whole Bible.* London: Oliphants, 1961.

LENSKI, R. C. H. *The Interpretation of St. Paul's Epistle to the Galatians, to the Ephesians, and to the Philippians.* Columbus, Ohio: Wartburg Press, 1946.

MEYER, F. B. *The Heavenlies.* Westchester, Ill.: Good News Publishers.

———. *Key Words of the Inner Life.* London: Morgan and Scott.

PAXSON, RUTH. *The Wealth, Walk and Warfare of the Christian.* New York: Fleming H. Revell Co., 1939.

PIERSON, A. T. "The Work of Christ for the Believer," *The Ministry of Keswick, First Series.* Grand Rapids: Zondervan Publishing House, 1963.

SCROGGIE, W. G. "Paul's Prison Prayers," *The Ministry of Keswick, Second Series.* Grand Rapids: Zondervan Publishing House, 1964.

WEBB-PEPLOE, H. W. "Grace and Peace in Four Pauline Epistles," *The Ministry of Keswick, First Series.* Grand Rapids: Zondervan Publishing House, 1963.

WILLIAMS, GEO. *The Student's Commentary on the Holy Scriptures.* Grand Rapids: Kregel Publications, 1953.

WRIGHT, W. C. *Ephesians.* Chicago: Moody Press, 1954.

WUEST, K. S. *Ephesians and Colossians in the Greek New Testament.* Grand Rapids: Wm. B. Eerdmans Publishing Co., 1957.